fala

Published under license from Editorial Gustavo Gili. *2G* was founded in 1997 as an international architecture magazine by Editorial Gustavo Gili, evolving, over the years, into a monographic magazine and international reference. Since 2016 it is published under license by Koenig Books.

Director and editor Moisés Puente

Graphic design RafamateoStudio

Translation Helena Antunes

Proofreading Paul Hammond

Cover photograph Ricardo Loureiro

Lithography Rovira Digital, Barcelona

Print agpograf impressors, Barcelona

First published by Koenig Books

Koenig Books Ltd
At the Serpentine Gallery
Kensington Gardens
London W2 3XA
www.koenigbooks.co.uk

Printed in Spain
ISBN: 978-3-96098-595-2

Distribution

Germany, Austria and Switzerland
Buchhandlung Walther König, Cologne
Tel. +49 (0) 221 / 20 59 6-53
Fax +49 (0) 221 / 20 59 6-60
verlag@buchhandlung-walther-koenig.de

Distribution outside the United States and Canada, Germany, Austria and Switzerland
Thames & Hudson Ltd., London
www.thamesandhudson.com

United States and Canada
D.A.P. / Distributed Art Publishers, Inc., New York
www.artbook.com

MIX
Paper from responsible sources
FSC® C104592

Contents

Rice and octopus

There are voices in Portugal saying that fala's position is too far from that of the Escola do Porto. True. The work of the young atelier does seem to represent the opposite of the architectures that have emerged around personalities like Fernando Távora, Álvaro Siza and Eduardo Souto de Moura, and that was apostrophized as representing a culture of "rice and octopus": simple but well-done, folk architecture at the highest level. Maybe the aforementioned voices are right: the conditions under which fala's works are created and perceived are completely different. Although Filipe Magalhães and Ana Luisa Soares have studied in Porto, and Ahmed Belkhodja has decided to live there, fala's network of good contacts, clients and friends is spread all over the world. And this also holds for the references fala is working with.

Tibor Joanelly is an architect and teacher. He studied Architecture at the ETH in Zurich and worked in several well-known Swiss architectural offices. Alongside his practice he has taught at Budapest University of Technology, the ETH and the University of Liechtenstein. He currently lectures on Architectural Critique at the University for Applied Sciences in Winterthur and he is an editor of the Swiss architectural magazine *werk, bauen + wohnen*.

A stack of old Japanese magazines

On the occasion of a visit to fala's atelier, Filipe placed a stack of old Japanese magazines on the table, magazines that Ahmed had brought back from a kind of safari through Japan. With Filipe and Ana Luisa, he shares an interest in the arrière-garde pupils of Kenzo Tange and Kiyonori Kikutake who won international attention with their experimental projects in the 1980s. Together with the early works of Toyo Ito, Kazunari Sakamoto, Takefumi Aida and Hiromi Fujii, they discovered the works of Itsuko Hasegawa, with whom Ahmed had a conversation not long ago. Hasegawa is a pupil of Kazuo Shinohara's, an architect whose name will be of some importance later on in this essay.

Against manual reason

Two floors above the atelier where Japanese magazines are flicked through one can find a "faulty corner" in a room next to the kitchen. It seems that in the apartment shared by Filipe and Ana Luisa, the contractor, while placing the formwork for the concrete of a slab, must have slightly mis-interpreted the position of a beam. A small prism of blank concrete now occupies one of the upper corners between the white plastered walls. For the fault to still be visible is the result of a veritable quixotism. The moment the wall below was finished and the fault became apparent, the builder proceeded to do everything he could to hide the blip with plaster—despite the architect's instructions to the contrary. And after the architects had tenaciously removed all the plaster, a painter again prudently covered up the "fault." Once again the architects had to remove everything… The faulty corner symbolizes the opposite of what a Central European might consider as incompetence: it was the result of perfection, of manual reason, typical for Portugal. Filipe knows how to tell many more stories like this: for the positioning of a pillar in front of a beam for spatial reasons, and not under it, regularly leads to disobedience if not revolt on the construction site. The same holds true for the positioning of drainpipes.

Against the client

Other windmills are tilted at in the relations with clients. In Portugal it is quite difficult to convince a client of the need for architecture because in building it is still common for most things to be done by the individual builder. An architect is only needed to sign the building application, meaning that architecture becomes a kind of martial art where the result is arrived at in a bout of speed, agility and deception. Working this way seemed at first sight to be unusual or even disconcerting for me and my Alemannic understanding of collaboration and professionalism, which includes a more or less close relationship with the client. But given the usual architect's fees in Portugal, a client cannot really expect more than a basic service. And an architect must not expect the client to understand his sophisticated language. Seen thus, expectations balance out.

Role models

In Portugal the business of architecture keeps to clear-cut role models and lifestyles. A column placed in the middle of a room would be interpreted as a design error and not as an architectural aim. fala is operating in a still homogenous social context. Hence their designs mostly keep to similar themes, spatially as well as in relation to the chosen material and the architectural elements that are used. And they also keep to an explicitly practiced thriftiness that reminds one of Adolf Loos. While the central hall in Filipe and Ana Luisa's apartment is in its own way a Shinoharesque exaggeration in size and symbolism, and even though the functions of the adjacent rooms are not really specified, the apartment follows a conventional plan.

Building without a design brief

Nevertheless, fala's projects may be characterized by a strong tendency towards autonomy. Or better yet, towards the emerging independence of architectural language. The development of a personal style—I think the term is correct here—is connected with another typical kind of commission. Many of the refurbishment projects in Porto were initiated by private investors trying to make a fortune through real estate speculation. After the economic crisis of 2008 the downtowns of Porto and Lisbon were confronted with a rampant boom in tourism. Speculation was propelled by special governmental measures such as the rescinding of far-reaching protection against dismissal or the easy availability of golden visas. In this context a client's brief is of only minor importance. A somehow generic tasking of basic domestic functions becomes even more generic when the project is considered by the client to be sold after completion. This may be the reason why some of fala's projects come across as topical declinations of the same program: the separation of auxiliary functions from the main space, the zoning of the plan, the opening and staging of the view onto a small courtyard.

Beyond zero tolerance

The protection of the city of Porto by UNESCO's world-heritage label led, within its expanded perimeter, to almost zero tolerance for any visible intervention. Design restrictions are so tight that even colors are prescribed. fala's handling of such constraints is quite creative and sometimes even tricky. In the Broken House, the architects simply interpreted the prescribed RAL-color with the NCS-system that delivered the finding that two different tones are possible within the given range. The two colors then became the base of the stripe pattern of the façade. Another norm in terms of fala's practice can be found in the way it treats the main façades of the many projects within Porto's first ring. The impossibility of contemporary expression is commented on by Filipe, who jokingly asserts that "the real main façades of our times are the ones towards the courtyard." Nowhere else does the remarkable theoretical volte-face become so clear as in the House in Paraíso, whose stripes on the courtyard façade made the office famous.

Square, circle, line

fala seemed to be an example of a current trend in architecture where geometric forms play a prominent role. One of the phenomena I wanted to investigate during my short visit to Porto was the circle that appears in most of the images that fala have created so far. Of course, I had in mind the circle in the gable end of the small enigmatic Tenmei House that Shinohara built in 1988. If in contemporary architecture the circle appears in many different correlations and contexts, in the works of fala it keeps to a certain history and purpose. This became evident with a glance at the court façade of House in Paraíso, the one with the green, black and white stripes of natural stone. It needed a decisive hint from Ahmed for me to understand why the brass circle hovered above the roofline slightly to the right of the central axis: it was there to guide the observer's gaze towards the upper right of the façade and to pull it away from the incidental and unhappy asymmetry caused by the neighbor's chimney. As a matter of fact the circle triggers a dynamic perceptual process like the one described at length by Rudolf Arnheim. Diversion, centering and releasing of the gaze is also provided by other "graphic" elements, such as the rectangular marble sheet on the upper right side of the garden façade of the Broken House. Its grid reminds one of the works of Peter Märkli and hints at the direction Shinohara could have gone in if he'd been more interested in the rules of perception.

Elements

fala has created a personal universe of forms and architectonic elements. Restrictions by a dearth of design briefs, tight budgets and the limited time available have meant that the three architects were forced to constrain, and in a certain sense to standardize, their design themes. Many of the architectural elements act like furniture staged in space, and this holds for cooking islands as well as for tiled surfaces or columns and dividing walls. Ana Luisa calls the resulting method of combining and recombining their own elementary and spatial vocabulary a "work with tropes." It finds a dazzling but also appealing expression in their new website, which is organized by themes rather than clear-cut projects: "main back façades, meaningful spaces, monochromes, pretentious kitchens, light-hearted pavements, careful mistakes."

Ongoing project

A logical consequence or merely the starting point of this working attitude is that the singular project loses its significant position within the oeuvre. Filipe, Ana Luisa and Ahmed see their work as a constantly ongoing and evolving project in which a non-realized idea can find immediate implementation in another commission—really in the manner of OMA/Rem Koolhaas: *Copy and Paste: How to turn a Dutch house into a Portuguese concert hall in under 2 weeks.*

Flat architecture

Given the importance of tropes, one could argue for an interesting difference with the work of Shinohara. Unlike the Japanese architect's aim of differentiating distinct projects by iconic names, the interior structure of fala's oeuvre is more rhizomic in kind, with like things appearing in different constellations on the surfaces of their designs. (Of course, such transverse relations can also be found in the oeuvre of Shinohara; but the Japanese architect tried to emphasize discreteness by the somewhat arbitrary marking of four styles). By playing down the differences between their projects, fala by no means follows the zeitgeist. And here the most significant difference with Shinohara becomes apparent. Seen from the perspective of today, the almost cult worship of the Japanese's oeuvre and person seems to be bound to a kind of feudal and patriarchal system of architecture, whereas Filipe, Ana Luisa and Ahmed see their practice as an open system in which they are just actors alongside their collaborators, clients, construction workers and others involved into their projects. In the language of network theory, they represent the nodal points where most of the connections converge. The flat hierarchy and organization are mirrored in the atelier, where everyone is sitting at the same table regardless of their function and position. The Japanese architecture critic Taro Igarashi once defined the works of such contemporary Japanese architects as Toyo Ito, Kazuyo Sejima, Atelier Bow-Wow and others as "superflat"—an attribute that also fits fala rather well. Although at first glance their works have next to nothing in common with the Japanese, they not only share with them a certain "surfaceness," but also the rejection of an accentuated hierarchy in expression.

Surfaces

Many of fala's projects are refurbishments and for now only a few of them go beyond setting new spatial constraints within a given structure. To keep costs down, new walls are often plasterboard balloon-frame-like constructions or made of non-loadbearing brickwork. The architects make no secret of these "superficial" techniques. But the eye takes these stagings of space for real and trusts the spatial tension that is built up between the animated elements. The play of surfaces makes for strong perceptual reactions, a kind of "spatial effect" that can be experienced corporeally via the eye: bulging and receding surfaces repel and attract. I use the expression "spatial effect" in reference to Roland Barthes's "reality effect" or to Gilles Deleuze's "effect of a literary machine"—and of course, I am also thinking of Shinohara's concept of the "wild space machine." Unlike the Japanese architect's designs, color plays a decisive role in fala's architectural compositions. Important parts are often lacquered, shining monochromes. The two-dimensional picture in space thus finds an equivalent in the collage-like images generated on computers; and as in space and on screen or paper, spatial effects emerge: for example, in the way wooden or stone elements are arranged economically (as in Álvaro Siza's works) as thin sheets, performing a kind of spatial mark-making. The nature of space becomes concrete when simple but elaborate processes of cutting and joining meet with more remote architectural elements—as on paper, performed with scissors and glue.

Order, projection

At first sight fala's works look like beautiful tableaux projected into space. Their spaces are designed in a pictorial manner, proceeding from surface effects, including pictorial composition and gaze-tracking, and ending by a call for the eye's active participation rather than the mere recognition of atmosphere. As in painting, compositions are primed with a geometric framework that sometimes becomes intelligible via observation and cognition. In many projects this framework is projected vertically over all the stories, defining a virtual roster that permeates the whole design. It becomes visible as a pattern in the flooring, embedding the different architectural and design elements in a united allover composition. It is this Eisenmanian structure that gives the designs a syntactic and profound raison d'être that goes beyond the perceivable effects of the surfaces. Although this structure is neither present as a literal spatial grid nor obliquely there through spatial transformation (as in the works of Peter Eisenman), it is capable of gathering the heterogenous elements in the composition as a syntax connecting pragmatic and semantic expressions.

Vernacular

In this way fala's architecture is decisively different to the typical older and younger "vernacular" architecture in the streets of Porto: it runs counter to the innumerable, samey, anonymous houses that were built in the 19th and the 20th century; the latter ones properly constructed and decorated with appealing tile patterns that emanate a happy Modernism. The difference holds because most of the façades speak with a reduced architectural language, being either pragmatic, as in the case of the older ones up to the 1930s, or with an emphasis on syntactic relations, as with buildings erected from the 1960s onwards (semantics was reserved for public buildings and buildings for the nobility). Walking through the streets of Porto with Filipe, Ana Luisa and Ahmed sharpens one's view of the constantly recurring details: a wooden lath on the top of a handrail or the canopy that conceals a saddle roof on the top of even the most modernistic building. Seen through the filter of these details, fala's architecture begins to look like an ennobled version of these graphic, colorful and playful façades: an anonymous Porto School…

Not naïve

It is quite probable that this affinity with the popular may have misled this or that critic to take fala's architecture to be "naïve"—a quality the three architects certainly flirt with when they speak of their work as a system of recurring elements or when they produce their Hockneyesque collages. But behind the great similarity of their projects a singular, complex network of relations, concepts and skills lies concealed. With that, a "Reminder to Architects" has to be made: Do not copy.

Post-possible Architecture

Pedro Bandeira

A consequence of the international recognition of "Portuguese architecture," mainly built around two Pritzker prizes and a School—the Porto School—was media attention over an extended consensus, structured on the idea of continuity, as if critiquing the ruptures promoted by the Modern Movement still made sense. While this laudatory consensus over "Portuguese architecture" presents itself as quite useful and, above all, exportable, it also represents an opportunistic simplification that seems to favor a deceptive moment of peace rather than the vigorous debate postmodern critique knew how to embrace (on behalf of eclecticism) and also, paradoxically, dispose of (by accepting relativism). We should probably begin by saying that fala can easily be seen in two different ways: abroad they are associated with a certain continuity within Portuguese architecture; in Portugal they are seen as disruptive, not to say unloved.

Pedro Bandeira (1970) studied Architecture at the University of Porto and is currently an associate professor at the School of Architecture of the University of Minho and a researcher member of Lab2PT. Author of several publications in the field of architectural culture, he is also co-editor of the *Fascículos de Fotografia* series published by Pierrot le Fou.

Even if we are still not sure of the end of the crisis in Portugal, the financial market and its ratings show that since 2015 there has been an economic recovery, a fact both pessimists and optimists concur with. A decrease in the rate of unemployment and an increase in exports are real proof of an economic upturn, but the emigration of well-qualified young people and an increase in strikes in the public sector reveal considerable social dissatisfaction, one that turns our crisis into our *fado* (fate)—a permanent condition, all but identity-defining. This is the pessimistic reading. The optimistic one is based on the increase in foreign investment motivated by the crisis, which left companies and assets in such a vulnerable situation that it made us question the real reason behind it. In addition, there is the exponential increase in tourism and the return of property speculation, motivated by a change in the Act on Rents, the golden visa project, and local housing's quick profits.

If we are to accept that these measures have somehow reversed the neglect and ruin towards the built heritage in the center of our cities caused by an exodus to their outskirts in the 1980s, it is also true that tourism associated with property speculation (with house prices only accessible to foreigners) is the basis of gentrification in Porto or Lisbon, which has revived people's claim to "the right to the city" theorized by Henri Lefebvre.

fala was to develop their activity, free from prejudice and with a high dose of optimism, in such an investment and speculation scenario.

But could they position themselves any differently? fala knew soon enough that if they were to open an architecture office they would have to adjust their service rendering to the contingency of the offer, by assuming that public contracts were scarce, and private ones, even though limited, were beginning to offer new opportunities, such as home renovation for local housing or property speculation. In most of these cases the client is a mere negotiator or mediator and not its usufructuary. Some of fala's clients are anonymous investors who do not even get to visit the houses they buy, a few of which even change owner several times without ever being inhabited. The initial sense of distress of not knowing exactly who you are working for, of having an abstract client, gave fala the freedom to think through the project in their own way, thus accelerating the creation of a few identity traits we shall address further on. The type of contract associated with local housing almost always entails a commitment to low-cost construction. Buying property for speculation may involve other budgets but in both cases the funding made available by clients is always low, considering the added value generated. Even the House with a Curved Wall, which was destined for a final client, was sold for five times more than the work itself, and the realtor was paid six times more than the architects. Once they became aware of this reality, fala tried to participate in the speculation game by themselves investing in a few projects. But in most cases, and in order to keep their office and collaborators working, they had to review their work methodologies in order to monetize their procedures by saving time and getting enough projects to make the office sustainable. This corporate logic expresses a discipline and rigor unusual in an emerging atelier, but still could not be considered as pure commercial practice. fala do not relinquish their romantic way of thinking that all contracts are legitimate regardless of their basic budget. This romanticism does not preclude an awareness of the value they produce, without a proportional return, in the speculative market. Paradoxically, however, the restrictions imposed by the speculative market are the same as the ones that allow them to reach less wealthy clients and charge 350 €/m^2. If, on the one hand we can say that fala's architecture perfectly portrays the yearnings of capitalist speculation, we should also acknowledge that it is more comprehensive from a social point of view. fala have managed to get the type of contracts architecture's star system tends to disregard—those within the middle and lower middle class.

They shamelessly agree to chop bourgeois houses of the 19th century up into one-bedroom houses, to transform garages into lofts, and *ilhas* (islands, typical Porto working-class housing) into student or tourist residences. What you cannot say, though, is that they do it only for the money: they do it, in the first instance, because they want to build and they see a rare opportunity to try out new housing typologies, which is evident in all their designs. That is also what distinguishes them from other anonymous commercial practices.

One could say that fala's way of doing things upstages criticism of the city in the midst of neoliberal transformation, and in that sense they take an apolitical stance on the world. Their discourse does not seem to contain any hint of ideology or morality and remains a humble attitude when compared to the heroic responsibility claimed by modern architects. fala are fully aware of their limitations and choose to claim their disciplinary knowledge alone without falling into the traps of social rhetoric. Aware of the world's complexity fala assume "a naïve architectural practice," a possible architecture, or better yet, one beyond the realm of the possible because they get to build a whole new imaginary.

As Fernando Távora once said, and not in a derogatory way, "Portuguese architecture has got a certain character. Why? Because it is shyer, more ignorant, less modern." All this was true—until the 1980s.

Even though they were too young to have lived through the euphoric years of the 80s, their practice still expresses, albeit inadvertently, a sort of throwback to a few theses we have identified as postmodern, either from a structural point of view, as a thought (an inevitability), or from a formal or stylistic point of view. It should be noted, however, that this return to postmodernism has nothing to do with nostalgia (you cannot feel nostalgic about something you did not experience): it results,

© Ricardo Loureiro

rather, from a reaction to a certain "minimalist" architecture, with all its simplistic morality vis-à-vis austerity in design, which has become a form of architectural "political correctness." On the other hand, fala's experience abroad (Switzerland, Japan and the United States) has stimulated a cosmopolitan culture which opposes the more conservative theses of those who advocate a "Portuguese architecture"—itself associated with a kind of morality of "the simple."

fala considered that a way to get around the laid-back view of what to expect and predict was to learn from the so-called "ugly ducklings"—an urban, anonymous, sometimes banal and at other times daring, yet always unsettling architecture. Following a methodology influenced by *Learning from Las Vegas*, fala have been developing several exercises (at Maia's Biennale 2019, TU Munich design studio and FH Münster) which allow them to balance their references to high and low culture. This positioning, legitimated by the postmodern condition, allows them to use the most erudite of architects and at the same time any other reference, wherever it comes from. This lack of prejudice explains the level of experimentation and differentiation we recognize in many of fala's projects, as well as a growing sense of irony (is the loose or dysfunctional pillar of the project House and Atelier a reference to Eduardo Souto de Moura's Market in Braga or to the unfinished works resulting from the economic crisis?).

The incorporation of both high and low culture also has a physical dimension that legitimizes the use of materials and solutions deemed to be less noble. Akin to what happens with the "ugly ducklings," we learn to do not what we want but rather what we can, without giving up on dignity and a certain joy. fala's creativity is mostly based on this quest for dignity, by transforming "trash" into "luxury" (see the attempt not to spend much and the creativity on the design of surfaces paved with patchwork marble, bought for 14 €/m^2, on the Broken House).

If it is true that they use postmodern eclecticism to create a balance between high and low culture, from a stylistic point of view the process is equally complex. Starting with the fact that fala themselves have declared a couple of years ago that they "do not have a building or graphic style."[1] This is a half-truth which can only be understood from two standpoints: the first is to think about style according to a wide set of references (a trend or fad) without assuming any particularity or specific place; the second is to consider these as the early stages of their work, a statement that will be betrayed by time and a wider range of buildings designed by them. We are just starting to recognize fala's building style via particular trademarks such as freestanding columns, circles on the façade, stripes or square patterns (which remind us of a certain 1980s postmodern architecture). The structure of postmodern thinking becomes pivotal once again to understanding a sense of style that falls between the complexity of a collective trend and the wish for a personal identity, which has gained ever greater importance. An aesthetic expression that

1 — See: Seixas, Diogo and Moreno, Joaquim, "A linha clara," *Jornal Arquitectos*, Lisbon, July 2014.

hardly falls into the "Portuguese architecture" category (in a contemporary vision revamped in order to secure media attention), which is not a bad thing per se—we would go as far as to say that advocating a "Portuguese architecture" is as simplistic an idea as the nationalist ideology that Salazar's dictatorship found in the *casa portuguesa* [Portuguese house] and *português suave* (a modern construction system combined with a nostalgic style).

One thing is for certain: postmodernism as a structure of thought had the virtue of encompassing all the apparent contradictions we are able to recognize in contemporary architecture (which allows us to mimic Álvaro Siza: "Functionalism in the morning and baroque in the afternoon.")[2]

The production of images in architecture has always had a multiplicity of goals, among which we may highlight the sense of representation. This representation can be seen in different ways, from the pragmatic representation of a project or building to the representation of an artistic or utopian idea. In any event, the image has become (mainly since the Renaissance) the first language of architecture and the architect has been recognized as an author. The rapport between the image and the idea of style is rather more complex. On the one hand the image was the determinant promotional vehicle of an architectonic style in a collective sense; on the other, and because it was conducive to the architect's expression as an individual, it was to be a causal factor of the erosion or apparent erosion of the idea of style. It was also because modernist architects upheld, albeit demagogically, the idea that "form follows function" that we stopped talking about style in architecture. The irony is that in all its diversity the Modern Movement itself did not resist the simplistic label of the International Style and the paradox of the mystification of a few of its protagonists by acknowledging their differentiation.

The legitimation of the architect-author (in the complex relationship between image, language, form and style) in the 1960s and 70s was much questioned. Architects were often accused of producing isolated objects, closed in their aesthetic dimension and unable to deal with several political and social issues (see the Situationist critique of the Modern Movement, particularly Le Corbusier). Simultaneously, architecture's disciplinary autonomy, its own knowledge related to the project and to its visual culture, was also questioned. Images should be able to stop being a thing in themselves (or simply disappear, legitimized by self-construction), or eventually the instrument of participatory processes.

Many architects at that time radically changed their disciplinary practice through their political activism, but others, without ever denying their convictions, knew how to balance their disciplinary autonomy (without excluding aesthetic issues and their identity as authors) through their response to social problems. Nowadays, this

2 — Expression used by Souto de Moura when referring to the period he worked with Álvaro Siza

balance is symbolically recognized in projects such as SAAL's Bouça neighborhood in Porto, designed by Álvaro Siza (and not by the people—their participation is a recurring mistake in the SAAL process). This particular case raises other questions because it was Siza's international recognition as a "star architect" that allowed them to finish and renovate the neighborhood after decades of degradation.

Álvaro Siza still belongs to a generation of architects—Aldo Rossi, Giorgio Grassi, Zaha Hadid, Peter Eisenman, Mario Botta, Frank O. Gehry, Steven Holl, etc.—who were granted the right to their own language, author-like, a fact which does not necessary exclude the interpretation of each work in a complex and phased way. This authorship was recognizable in many buildings (in their aesthetic choices), but also in images per se; that is to say, images not connected to the need to communicate a project. Pen sketches, watercolors, oil paintings or colored pencil drawings that represented imaginary landscapes, angels or horses obtained media attention in a way that went beyond the realm of architecture.

Nowadays one cannot say that the "star system" is nourished by the coherence that seemed to underlie the architect's authorial language, partly because postmodern thought, with all its relativism, has freed architects from the necessity to be coherent and, on the other hand, because increasing visibility in the media associated with a marketing strategy calls for a permanent competition for distinction. Consequently, architecture evolved in the sense of feeding this show with ever more iconographic buildings, but also with the spectacularization of the architects themselves, who were increasingly subjected to media pressure. In that sense architects are no longer just "authors" (a condition inherent in the image of their work) but also "personae" (a condition inherent in their self-image).

But the excess of images in circulation through the different media makes it easier to lose sight of their references, which may lead to diversion or *détournement* (according to the Situationists), instigating an unlimited appropriation legitimized by postmodern relativism. This absence of limits hinders an idea of style or at least fragments it in a fractal-like manner. At the same time the excess of images leads to an inevitable redundancy based in part on "coincidences" from which there emerges the will to understand a broader sense of style, such as, for instance, the idea of the post-digital, where fala could perfectly fit in.

fala's postmodernism takes us to the post-digital as a representational practice, which brings us back to a pre-digital aesthetic influenced by Henri Rousseau or David Hockney's paintings. The images produced by fala have something naïve and pop about them, as if they were trying to explain their architecture to children, even though the drawings are useful for conveying information about the execution of the work in communicating a minimum of data about the project to ill-prepared builders. Such images also try to demonstrate the simulated appropriation of everyday life by using common objects, plants, books on the floor, clothes hanging on doors. The habitability of these homes is almost always treated as something fleeting, with someone who has just arrived or is preparing to leave, but there is always time enough to portray a certain intimacy.

We recognize the language of the images together with the work developed by other studios (OFFICE Kersten Geers David Van Severen, Baukuh, Point Supreme) but in fala's case there is this persistence, which has two complementary yet opposed readings: one is related to the image per se; the other is its disquieting proximity to the built work.

We might say that fala gained recognition even before the revelation of their built work—which only recently began to get some exposure. Encouraged by social media, the primacy of the image is the only possible strategy for studios that have just embarked on their activities, even though in most cases the efficacy of the images is utterly ephemeral. Nevertheless, fala's graphic persistence and coherence in terms of representation has granted them international visibility. In that respect, and judging by the success of their images, we may claim that fala have built their identity on the latter, in keeping with a tradition in which representation is an autonomous discourse (because it is independent of the work) and legitimizes authorship. Yet even though in the case of other architects this autonomy was used to free architectonic discourse from the work's materiality (by exploring utopias and imaginary constructs), fala took it as a disquieting convergence of the images and the work or, better yet, of the work and the images—in a complete reversal of direction. If we say disquieting and not expected (this must be the direction of representation) it is because as far as fala are concerned they (the work and representation) blend almost irrepressibly. fala's images are not coded designs, they are not vehicles that lead to the work's materiality, they are a place of their own and it is the work that meets the images, it is the work that dematerializes in order to become image by imitating its lightness. In that sense the chance to annul the distance and time between image and work is evoked—the very representation of utopia.

We could name several other studios in which digital representation, or rendering plausibility, favor the same fusion between image and work, but they seldom consider the image as the endgame. The work becomes the image, in a naïve sort of way, as we were given the opportunity to see, which is also a critical positioning about an "idea of perfection" promoted by the exactness of digital technology and by the architectonic visual culture which comes from simple forms.

fala's architecture gives the world back its poetry, with all its complexity and imperfection, an awareness only possible through its representation.

The Pictures Generation

Kersten Geers

The 'social media' revolution happened without me noticing it.

Virtual reality got solidified through collage-like images; snapshots of possible worlds.

When I was confronted with some of these *pictures*, scooped up from a parallel digital universe, I had no real opinion about them. I guess their immediate recognizability provoked only some kind of mild indifference. The ingredients looked familiar, the compositions sophisticated; an accumulation of tropes of good painterly taste. Was there any space, beyond the plants and the cool figures? Was there any *architecture*? I guess raising the question implied knowing the answer. Still, undeniably the social networking had overthrown the conventions of relevance and reached even the otherwise conservative firmament of architecture.

Kersten Geers (1975) studied at the University of Ghent and at the Madrid School of Architecture (ETSAM). He worked in Rotterdam for Maxwan/Max.1 Architects and for Neutelings Riedijk Architects, and in 2002 he founded OFFICE Kersten Geers David Van Severen together with David Van Severen. He has been a tutor at the TU Delft, the University of Ghent and the Accademia di Architettura di Mendrisio, and a guest lecturer and guest critic for the Berlage Institute in Rotterdam, and Columbia University in New York, among other institutions. He is a founder-member and editor of *San Rocco* magazine, and frequently publishes essays on architecture in a variety of magazines and books. In 2008 the practice was awarded the Belgian Prize for Architecture and in 2010 with the Silver Lion at the 12th Venice Biennial of Architecture.

A few years ago fala's perspectives appeared among the similar visual multitude on the internet—suddenly: confident, complete. There were some reasons to doubt both the coherence and the depth of the message, let alone the profundity or even the "intentions" of the messengers. What were they selling us: a hypothetical good universe constructed from fragments of "good" objects? *Life with objects* after a few decades *without*?

Radical architectural positions often find refuge in the two-dimensional world of flat representation. The view, the perspective, is traditionally used as a window to a hypothetical world: a projection. Images travel fast and are a powerful means of communication. This is an old idea. This was already true during the last century (and in fact many centuries before). Pamphlet and poster-like messages presented a possible architecture, shortcutting the need to detail the proposal and even the urge to build (often for good).

However, judging fala's images from that perspective—which I initially did—gets you nowhere. Despite their appeal, the purpose of the images is much less clear. What do the pictures reveal? Where is the provocation in this celebration of immaculate good taste? As radical architectures they fail to convince. fala makes pictures not to communicate, but to exist. The medium is the message. They realize (I believe consciously) that perspectives are perspectives, images in their own right; a pitch for a possible architectural experience, not some sort of announcement of a revolution.

In 1979, the New York art critic Douglas Crimp republished an essay called "Pictures" in the journal *October.* The revised text was a simplified and slightly altered version of a catalogue entry that had accompanied an exhibition at Artists Space in 1977, showing six young artists who were loosely working with similar reproductive techniques. In the second edition of the text, the group of artists in focus had significantly altered. The new group thus presented a generation of artists able to confront the then omnipresent literal minimalists: they became the *picture generation.* The initial show was visited by few. The text, and thus the collection of artists, acquired relevance in its second incarnation. Crimp seemed to argue that post-Donald Judd, and post-Michael Fried's criticism of both the literal and the theatrical, a new art was emerging that celebrated the (film) still as an unfinished picture "whose existence never exceeds the fragment," and thus embraced a certain theatricality, but avoided the potential pitfalls with its pseudo-casualness. The "picture" as a *still* of a non-existent film is incomplete, fragmentary. In Cindy Sherman, Robert Longo and Sherrie Levine's work, the incomplete, the fragmented and the appropriated all played a role in equal parts. Looming over each of them was the great formal conceptualist John Baldessari, who was in hindsight their biggest influence and trailblazer. Sherman, Longo and Levine presented a generational shift in the way the "picture" was valued. All of a sudden the picture itself was considered a direct conceptual image: in flux, yet autonomous. In Crimp's thinking, these art practices introduced a "postmodern" art, self-ironical, aware of its own artifice and inability for closure. The art was then radically contemporary, and the incomplete *artifice* more successful in representing the issues and ambiguities in society than any earlier literal and complete attempt (of making art) was able to. That was 40 years ago.

The artifice runs deep in the practice of fala. In strict terms, the office often makes an architecture that seems completely unnecessary. The space they transform is often already there, the transformation is seemingly cosmetic. In this ambiguity, perhaps, there lies an important quality of their work. Making the existing more beautiful is a strategy. It makes the space "exist." Visiting many of the transformed properties in Porto provoked an exchange about the dynamics of buying and selling in relation to the places fala transforms. The added graphic quality of the transformed spaces often acts as a memory clue in the commercial transaction. After having visited several real-estate opportunities possible buyers simply remember the spaces fala transformed better. As a result several investors gave increased freedom to the architects to pursue their graphic and spatial experiments. Architectural success here miraculously follows commercial success, or vice versa. Apart from freedom the architects gain little, however; budgets are small, fees are low. Still, the heated market seems ironically to create a niche that is intelligently abused by fala for an architecture that only exists because, or in parallel to, its own image. The photographs of their work, taken with just as much care as their collages, play a similar ambiguous and decisive role. They present a ghost of spaces that due to a quick change of ownership often become quickly inaccessible.

In the last decade, in the aftermath of the financial crisis in Portugal, thousands of affluent foreign people have been lured to the capital and its vicinities through a cunning—yet in the long term destructive—tax proposal. This "citizenship for money" scheme created an instant surge in property, first in Lisbon and now, in its wake, in Porto too. French money ran smoothly into the country, with the promise of no more taxes for those who take up citizenship. In no time at all a wealth of foreign investment transformed both cities. Houses that were forever dilapidated suddenly became hot property. Garages could become flats. Small workers' row houses could be worth a fresh look and an intelligent investment. An architectural boom never happens without an economic opportunity, and Porto is no exception to that rule. In the slipstream of an abundance of terrible projects for money, either for people who move in, or those who simply invest and sell, a few smart practices try to make the best of it and tweak this tricky condition into an opportunity. In order to do so, however, one has to rethink what architecture could be about. Or better yet, what it could still be about when its primary necessities are economy and visual persuasion. Is there still a project, after these themes are seriously considered? Or are they the project proper?

The projects of fala were initially born in the context defined by the popular house-sharing apps. In the shadow of the big financial takeover of Lisbon, people

with a bit more ambition and less money started to buy, transform and sell simple properties in central Porto. The spaces that are found and finally bought are unusual. They are urban leftovers: half-plots, garages, semi-buildings, quasi-cellars. These unusual spaces require unusual spatial solutions. If you transform a garage into a residence it does not become a conventional house with three separate bedrooms. fala somehow realized that the only way to transform these spaces into something interesting is to accept their spatial principle and to idealize. To project on each of them a fragment of a spatial type, without being too preoccupied with the spatial purity of each of these. Type is here approached from a perspectival point of view, and thus replaced by an image of a type: a picture. With wit and bravura they transformed a tunnel garage into a tunnel-like "house" with side rooms behind a meandering wall. The main space is long and weird and photogenic. The small spaces are dark but still practical. The whole is a radical spatial constellation where the standard spatial quality norms do not apply and are therefore exciting. Economy and enticement bring about spatial invention. The seemingly impossible spatial constellation of the original place is unconditionally embraced and turned into its advantage. It somehow helps that these residences are often sold as secondary homes. Homes with little or no rules, spaces to experience and convince. Through fala's cunning, speculation is tweaked into an engine for an architectural project. This curious association between economy and unusual spatiality has a particular ancestor in Japanese housing architecture of the late 1980s and early 90s. It is an association eagerly made by fala themselves. It makes you see the unusual nature of the rooms of their projects as a belated offspring of Itsuko Hasegawa's economical formalisms or Toyo Ito's early private houses. Each of them in their own right sought formal and spatial freedom, away from the traditional Japanese house, towards three-dimensional spatial experiments, by means of two-dimensional figuration. Considering these architects tried to deconstruct the traditional house in the period of exceptional economic prosperity, one cannot help but see an odd parallel in fala's contemporary mannerism. As portrayals of the Portuguese boom their projects measure the possible in a context sickened by commercial imperatives.

During my visit to some of the fala buildings and buildings in the making, we drove to the city of Marco de Canaveses. There were a few reasons for this: one of the partners grew up in the vicinity, a square house with a curious plan, the House for Three Generations, was about to be finished in a neighboring village, and Álvaro Siza's church in the old town was worth a visit. The road from the square house to the church made us pass by a traditional barn with a pitched roof and the ruin of a baroque palazzo; a gigantic façade that was never finished. Both buildings were located a few hundred meters from each other. There they were, as the improbable ancestors of fala's architecture: a decorative front, a display of "architectural intentions" and a simple spatial type, compact and ideal but inaccessible. One surface-only, one volume-only.

After Siza's church we went to see a second house, the House under a Big Roof, under construction. A massive beam on top of the long side of the building seemed to keep a pitched roof in place. Although the house looked a bit like a clumsy emulation of a house, it was the surreal façade composition—a highly inventive window-door constellation sharply off-center, a pilaster-like column left, the beam on top—that took all the attention. The House for Three Generations we visited earlier that day was a masterpiece of spatial economy: no form, only volume, barn-like. As a square container with a slightly pitched roof, the figure of the building revealed little of the spatial complexity inside. The plan was simple yet effective. The square plan (inside) was mutilated by individual cells (like micro-houses) located in three of the four opposite corners. Each cell had a particular formal identity. Their geometry defined a shared collective space through subtraction. In this shared space a "fake" column was added slightly off-center for spatial effect. It provided the place with a point of gravity, a reference point. With a few gestures another world, slightly disconnected from the actual *place*, emerged.

While we were leaving the house, waiting for the architects caught up in a complex discussion with both the contractor and the parents of the clients, a Portuguese couple that lives and works in Switzerland, I noticed the railing circumventing the full perimeter of the site, like a fence. It felt as if the village had to be protected against the presence of the house itself, a job the railing did with conviction. The house thus remained foreign to its own current location. To me it read like a metaphor for fala's actual operation, that of often making architecture in the heart of Portugal with foreign money and radically simple spatial ideas and a certain ambivalence towards its actual context: *Fremdkörper* in the heartland of the Portuguese school.

Back in the office in Porto we looked at a cardboard model of a collective housing block in a small village, away from Porto, on which construction was soon to begin. Buildings and sites have recently become so expensive in the city of Porto that investors have started to seek other opportunities away from the city. They hope to develop housing projects with other users in mind.

The project for the collective housing is deceivingly simple. A rectangular volume with more or less regular windows, balconies where needed, *porte-fenêtres* where affordable: a building as the purest incarnation of an economy of means. Inside the volume, the architects designed a relatively complex spatiality, defining the separate units in a way reminiscent of the spatiality "found" in the urban transformation projects in central Porto. These unfinished spatial types were simply internalized in the housing volume and created a set of geometrically complex units that together added up to the simple housing volume. Technically, the scheme was simple. The outer envelope was the main structure; internally the walls created a set of distinct apartment plans. The only other frivolity the architects allowed themselves was a frieze made of triangles, semi-circles and circles, painted on the outer walls of the building volume. It gave a strange illusion of a semi-coherent, quasi-systematic abstract façade: a picture on a big box.

House for Three Generations, Marco de Canaveses

2015-

The house stands in a corner plot of a small Portuguese village; it is meant to house three generations of the same family. Each generation is assigned a private space with a different shape; the given shapes are apparently arbitrary yet extremely precise. The communal living area is the negative of the private spaces and presents an unorthodox form. The relation between private and public programs induces a domestic environment that is almost obscene (in the theatrical sense of the word).

The house has a square plan and a pyramidal roof; its corners point in the cardinal directions. Along the five equally important elevations, one finds a continuous texture of exposed gray concrete, white painted concrete, large square windows and smaller round windows. The metal chimney ends the object, holding it together.

Like most houses, this one is made of rooms, windows, doors, floors and white walls. Somewhere in the living area a rough column is added and all the wooden floors are laid in a centrifugal manner from it, marking the separation between different common activities. Although nearly central, the column is not structurally necessary and, as such, doesn't touch the ceiling. Incidentally, the column acts as a punctuating device, serving as a hint to the physical unity of the house, a concrete square in the middle of the world.

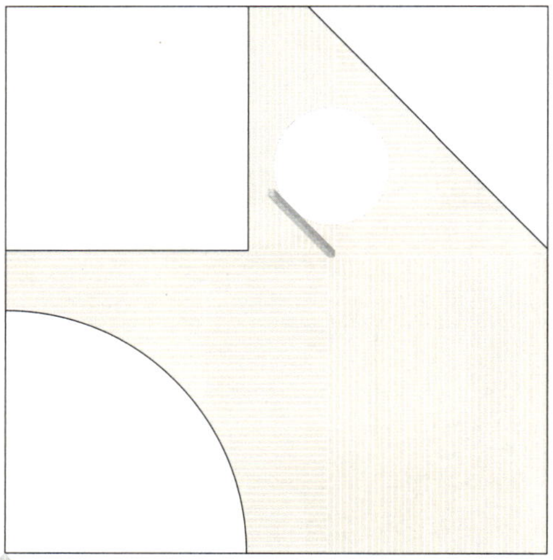

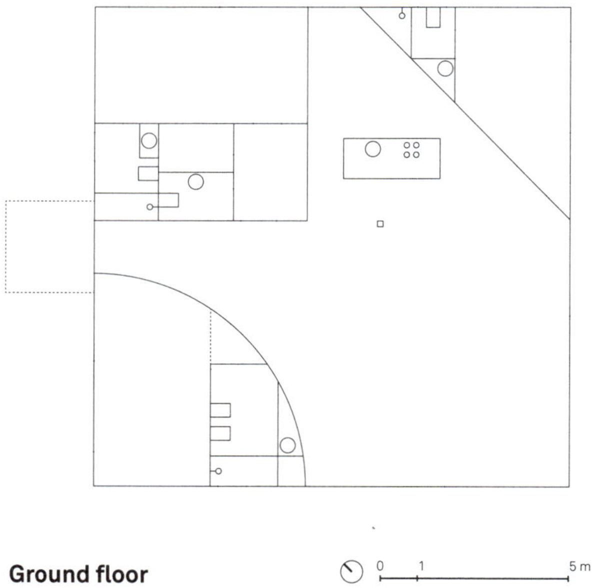

Ground floor

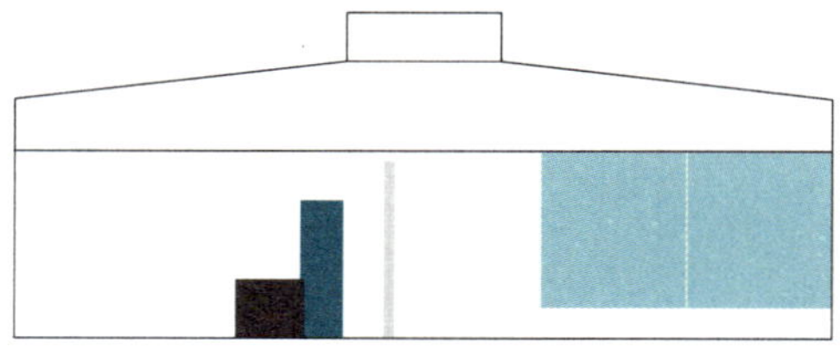

Section

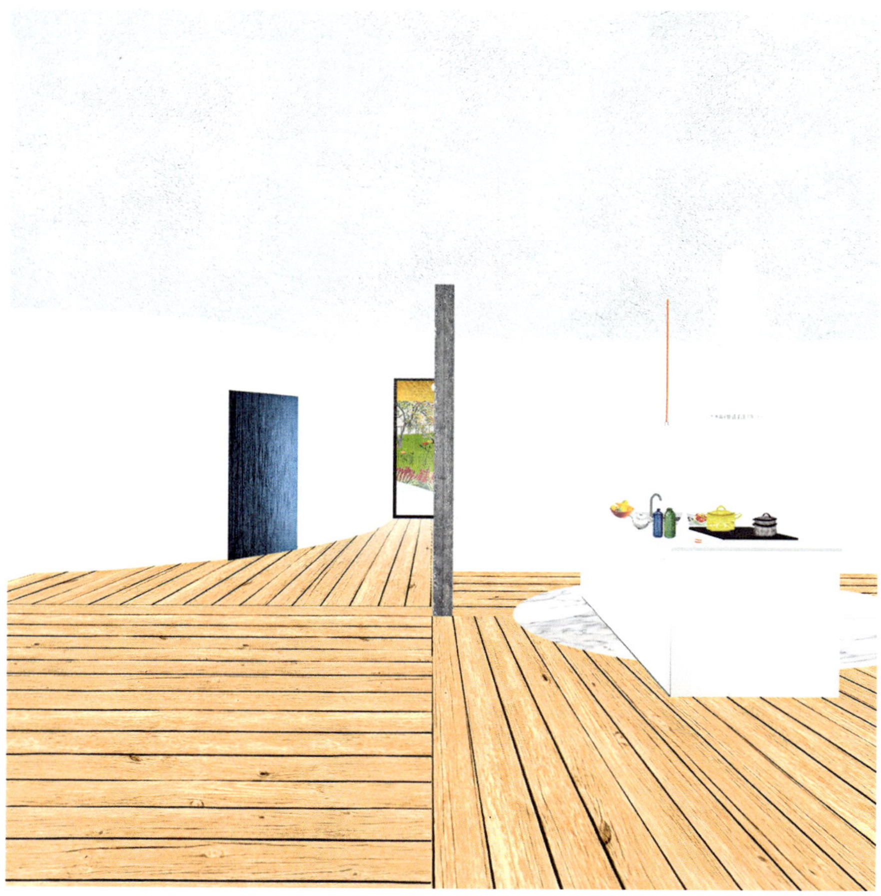

House in Paraíso, Porto

2016-2017

A bourgeois 19th-century house is divided into four identical living spaces sharing a private backyard. The project unfolds within a given system of constraints, aiming at an unexpected complexity, finding interest within a very banal set of decisions.

The front façade is almost unchanged. The shabby tiles are replaced by polished green marble contrasting with the roughness of the existing granite frames. Only a circle of white marble is added to balance the composition.

Unorthodox everyday spaces are built according to a clearly defined syntax and grammar. The four living rooms are different from each other while sharing the same language, the same set of figures: the stepped wall, the curved surface, two doors (one pink and one green), a striped wooden floor.

The back façade is rebuilt. It becomes taller to match the neighbors' scale, like a mask or a temple, with two square windows framing interior scenarios. The polished surface has a bold pattern of vertical stripes assembled with white, green and black marble, creating a rich, yet flat, exterior appearance. The entrance door is hidden within the pattern; a brass circle on top ends the piece. The pattern disguises both the scale of the building and its program while being unnecessarily exuberant. The back façade becomes a painting for neighbors to look at, a main façade for private use.

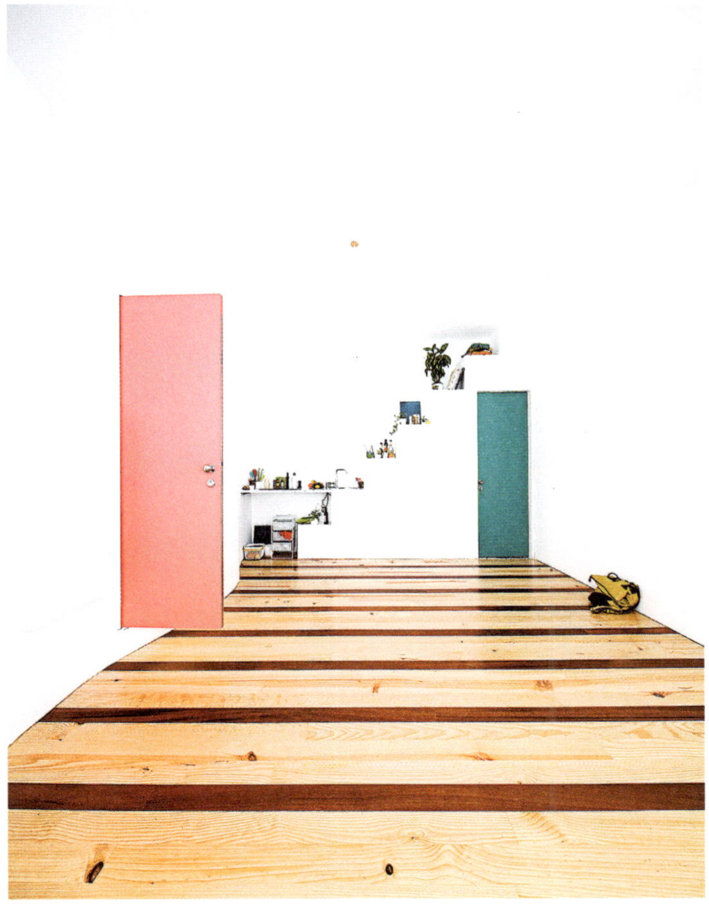

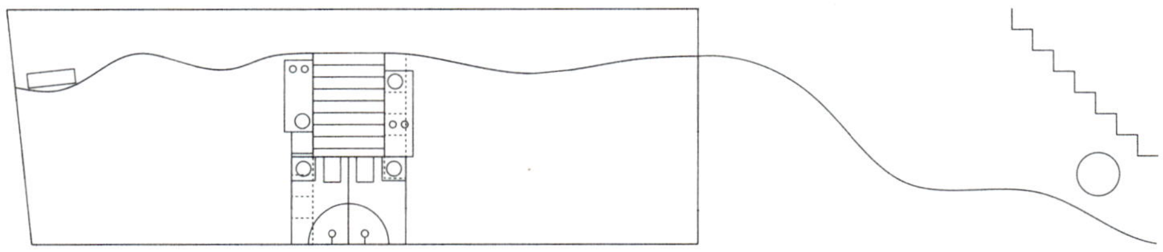

Ground floor

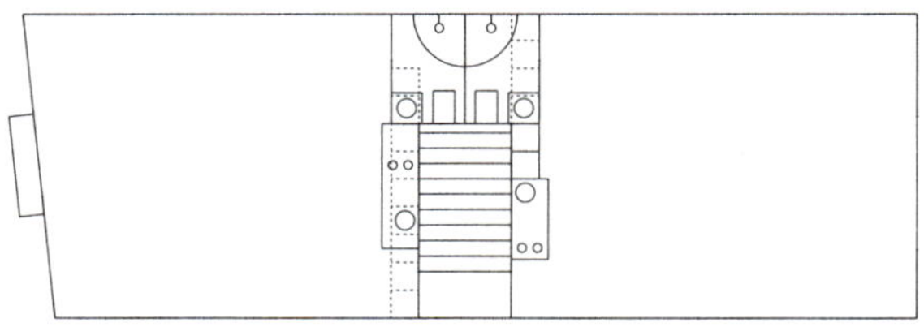

First floor

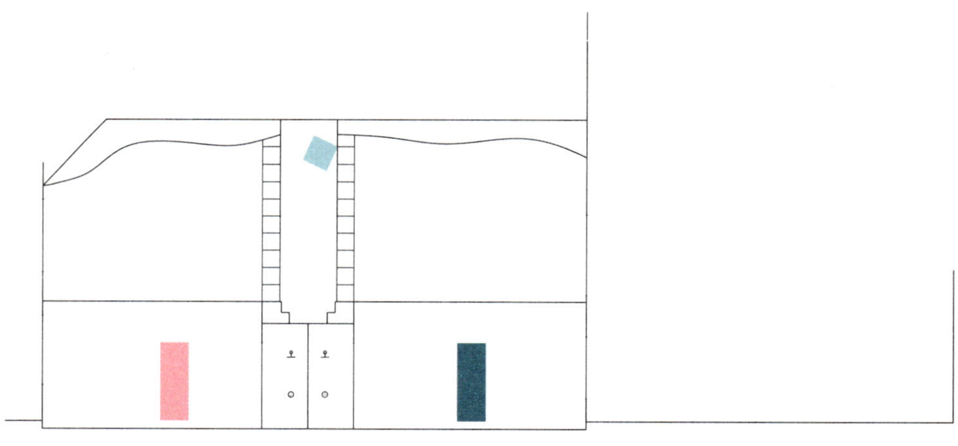

Longitudinal section

Reasonable Housing, Penafiel

2016-2018

Within a quiet suburban village of vernacular detached houses, the factory that acted like a house was transformed into an apartment block that resembled the factory that never was. The building lives in archetypal innuendo.

Each of the three levels is comprised of two apartments in which the extremely low budget imposed very low standards for the construction. Nevertheless, the proposed open plan granted generous areas and various orientations in all apartments, creating a spatial tension between an imposed scarcity of means and a certain spatial luxury.

The geometry of the plan starts from the existing alignment of columns. The axis, off-centered due to the different sizes of the machines that originally occupied the space, provided a grid; from that point, geometry ruled over the general arrangement. Six square rooms, one of them divided in two triangular spaces, a curve, and a small kink. Rules, exceptions, and unbalanced symmetries were imposed to achieve an order. A sequence of equally distanced blue doors aligns with the existing concrete columns and a brutal beam to create a sense of continuity.

The façade is simple and ordered, following rules dictated by the plan. An apparently regular grid of identical windows stresses the purity of the white volume; the drainpipes are disposed in an exuberant manner, to unbalance the composition. The fake cornice, the roughness of the white texture, the repetition of the same opening and the domestic blue door marking the building's common entrance hold an architectural language of playful restraint

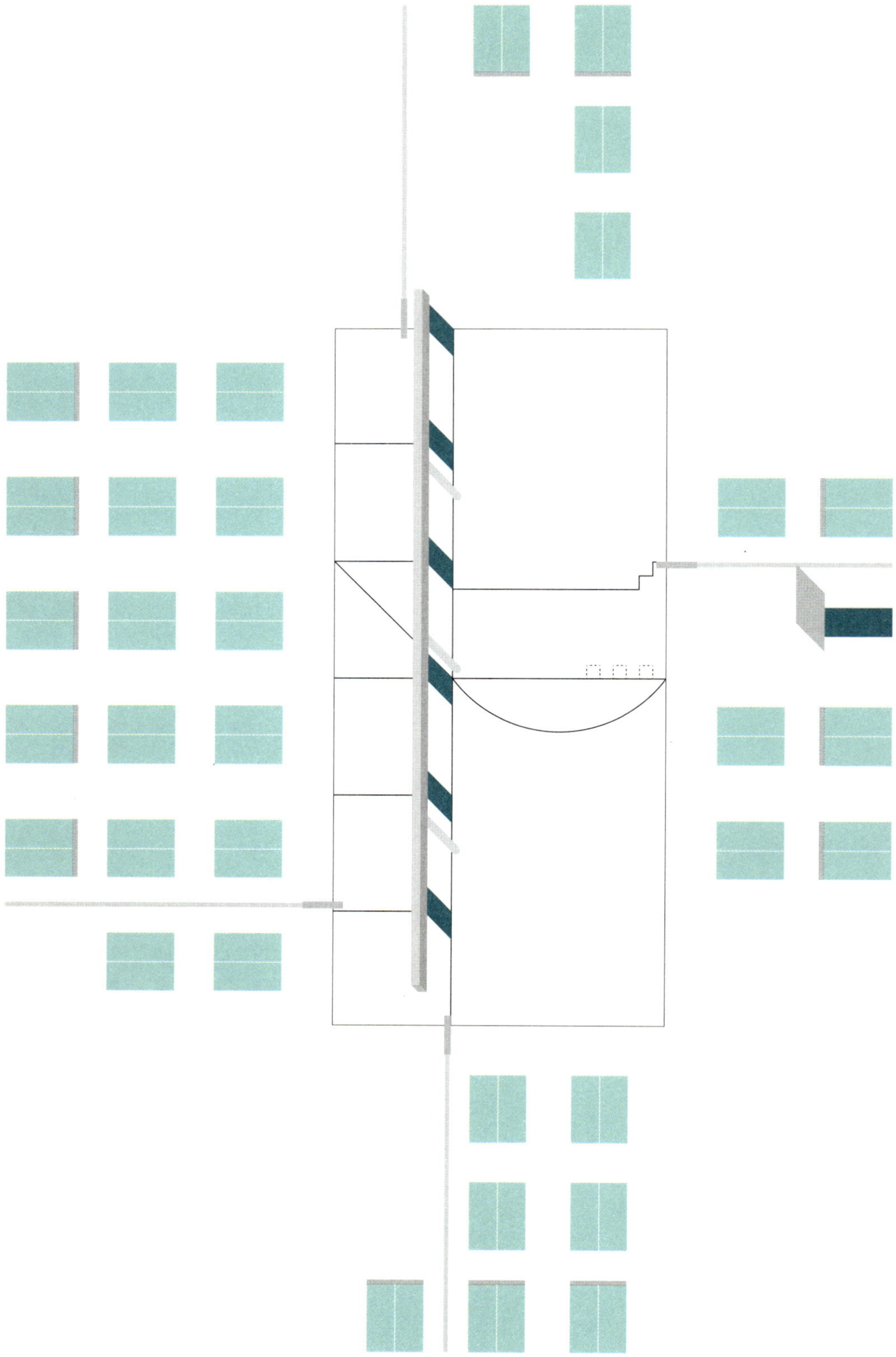

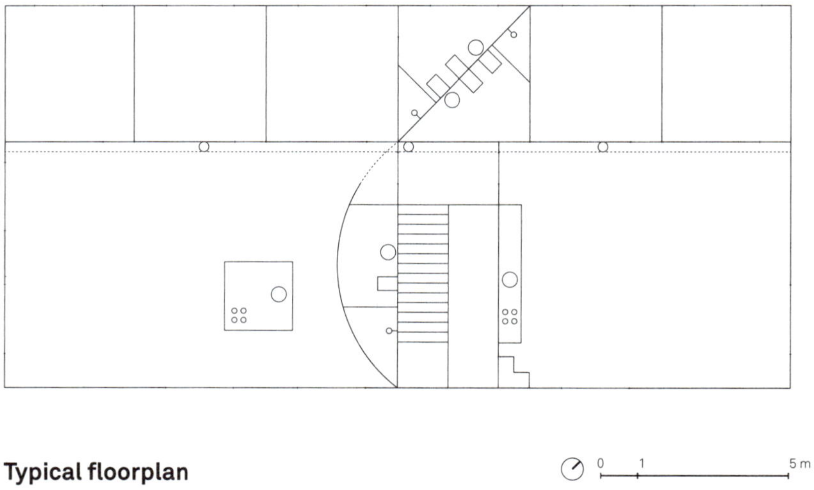

Typical floorplan

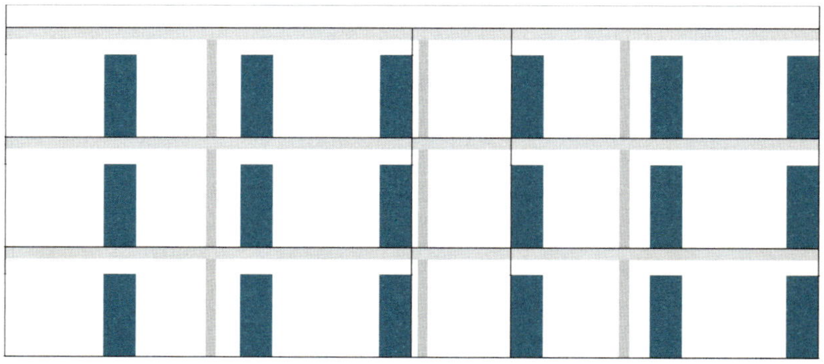

Longitudinal section

House in Fontaínhas, Porto

2016-2019

A clear division between public and private programs was requested. The project is structured within overlapping antagonistic orders.

The ground floor is conceived as one uninterrupted space defined by a free curved wall. It is a volatile room with only one corner and two continuous white surfaces opening up to the vivid garden. Its inner elevations are carefully calculated. Conversely, the first floor is a composition of intricate rooms and rhythmic collisions of different geometries, a sequence of irregular spaces. The complexity is introduced to accommodate all the necessary programs, adapting to the narrow perimeter of the site. A set of equally distanced wooden beams supporting the roof causes inconvenient intersections.

In contrast with the opposing spatial orders, materiality holds the house together. Fluent white walls are stuck between striped wooden floors and light blue ceilings, disturbed once in a while by flat blue doors, touches of marble or a pink kitchen.

The back façade didactically reflects the three orders. The ground floor is completely open to the garden while on the first floor a single window frames a certain perspective of the peculiar context. The striped concrete cornice is introduced on both elevations and a blue circle, aligned with an unnecessary pink column, ends the peculiar composition.

A ground floor dissolving into the garden, a precisely divided *piano nobile*, a headstrong roof.

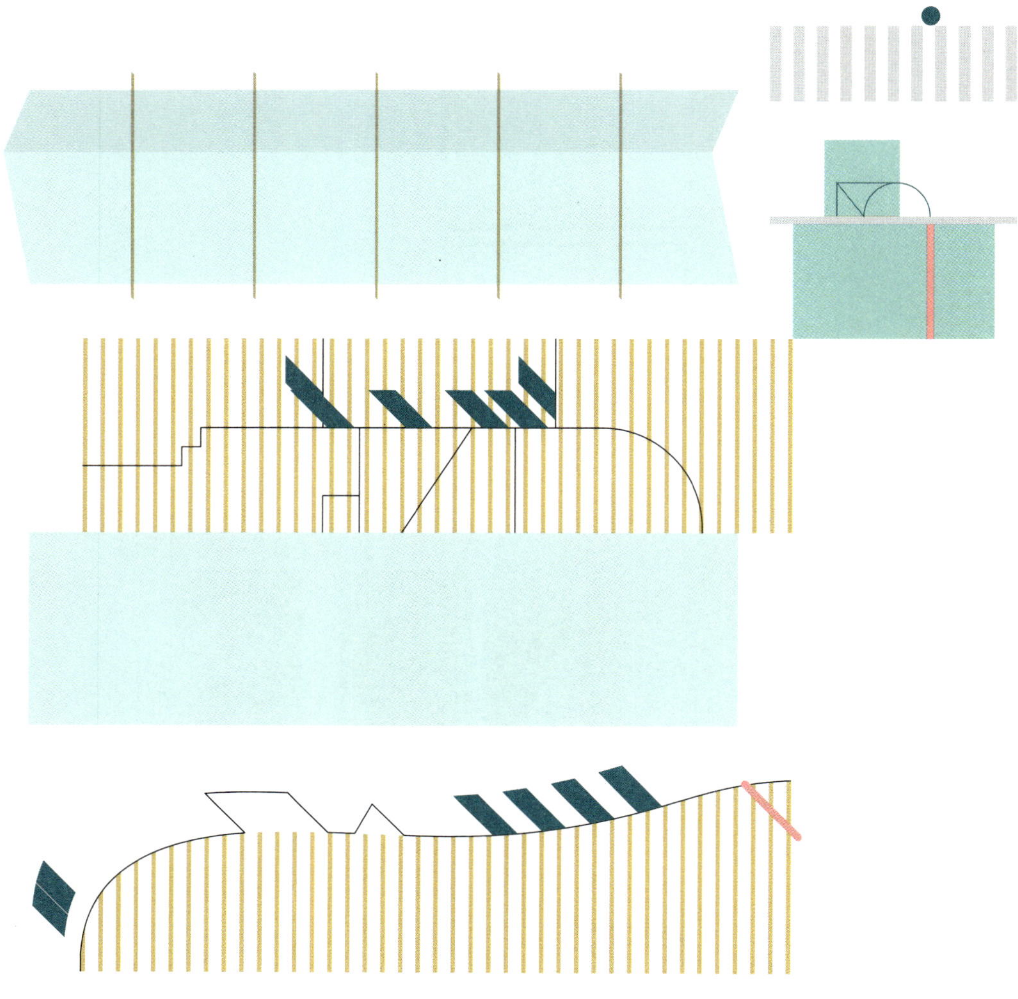

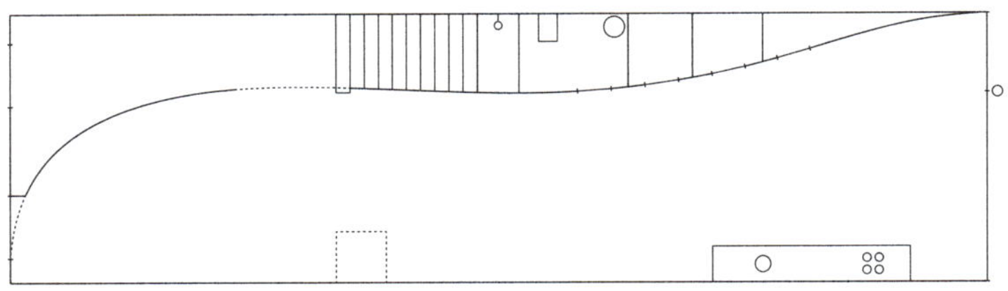

Ground floor

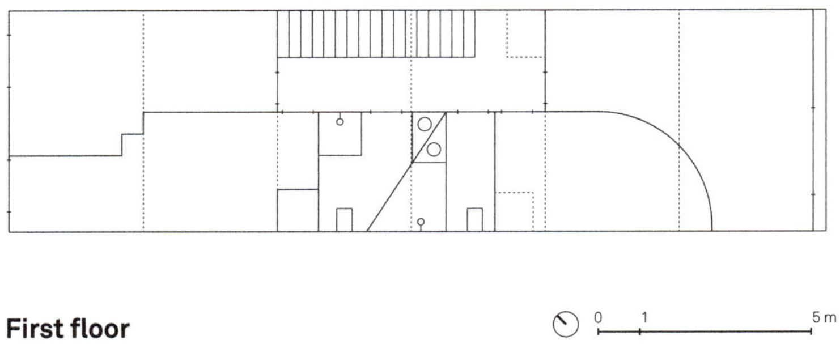

First floor

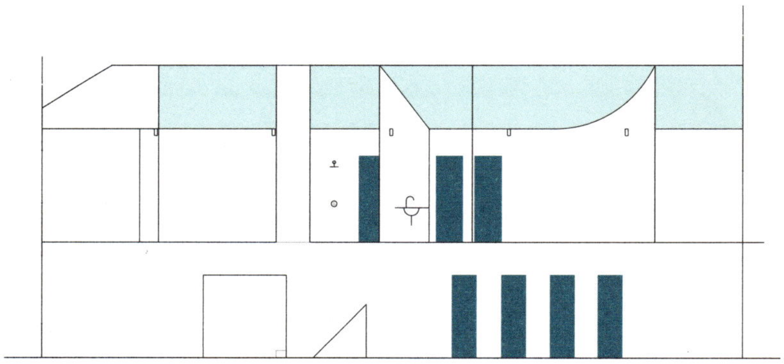

Longitudinal section

House with a Curved Wall, Porto

2016-2017

Within an extremely low budget, the decrepit original construction was reset to the bare structural existence of its perimeter walls.

The inner space was solved with the precise placement of a gently curved wall as a separation between the public and private programs under a new light roof. The intersection of the existing perimeter walls, the sloped ceiling and the added curve resulted in a complex geometrical form. A sequence of rooms of various sizes and forms hides behind the new wall and a wide window frames the rediscovered garden.

The main space, loosely populated by furniture, showcases four blue doors, a circular opening, various plants and a slender metal pole that symbolically marks the highest point of the otherwise humble construction. A selected number of elements were painted in strong colors contrasting with the general abstract whiteness of the room.

The wall facing the street was extended to balance its proportions and the entrance door painted in heavy salmon-pink; the greenish-blue gate, when closed, completes the deconstructed composition. A thin metal surface extends over the white volume as if made of paper: the light metal roof becomes the prominent urban element defining the image of the house, its "houseness."

While the interiors form a unity characterized by whiteness and precision, the outside expression is that of a loose juxtaposition of constructional elements. Ultimately the house is a rather conventional building, but unusually vivid.

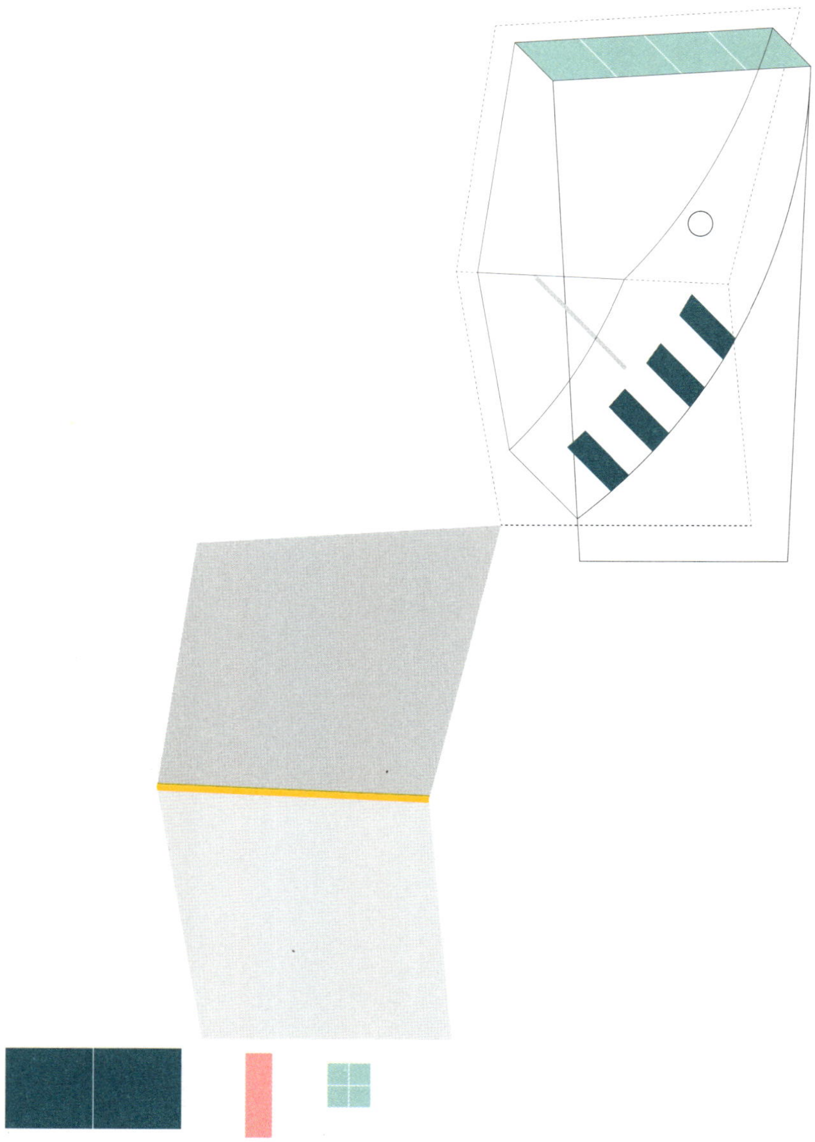

House with a Curved Wall, Porto

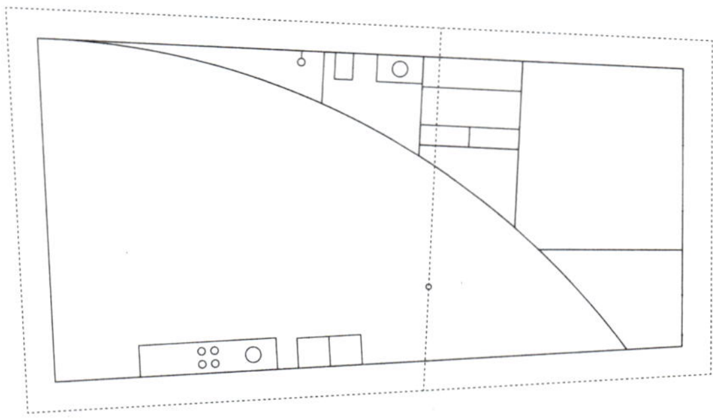

Ground floor

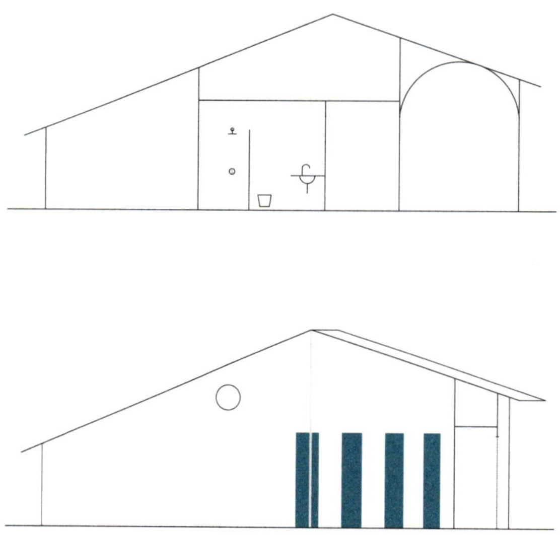

Longitudinal sections

House with Four Columns, Porto

2016-2018

The lofty 19th-century house stands in a narrow alley in front of a cemetery. The project pursued a certain sense of an absolute order.

The existing wooden structure was replaced with concrete and an unspoken grid redefined the geometry of the plan. The central core of the staircase, two triangular bathrooms on each level, four relatable living spaces, and a slightly curved corridor on the ground floor organize the necessary uses and hierarchies. Every room is conceived as a white perimeter punctuated with a concrete column in the very center, establishing a certain order of programs, hinting at a way of inhabiting the space, making the space understandable. The given columns are architectural devices, non-structural and, as such, they don't touch the ceiling.

Each living room becomes an assembly of banal figures: the two blue doors, the practical marble surface, patches of tiles, movable cabinets, and windows facing opposite exterior scenarios. The exercise in materiality, bringing together wood, concrete, tiles and marble, seamless surfaces and patterns, felt necessary. The garden gets underway covered in white tiles and blossoms between the pre-existing perimeters of white walls.

Each elevation tells a different story. The front façade is austere, covered with banal white tiles, dominated by two tall doors, one pink and one blue. The side façade is defined by three thick painted lines, reflecting the inside structural composition. The nonfigurative garden façade is composed of two square windows and a drainpipe disposed within a nonconformist silhouette. The side wall of the neighbor is painted in dark blue, enhancing the autonomy of the piece.

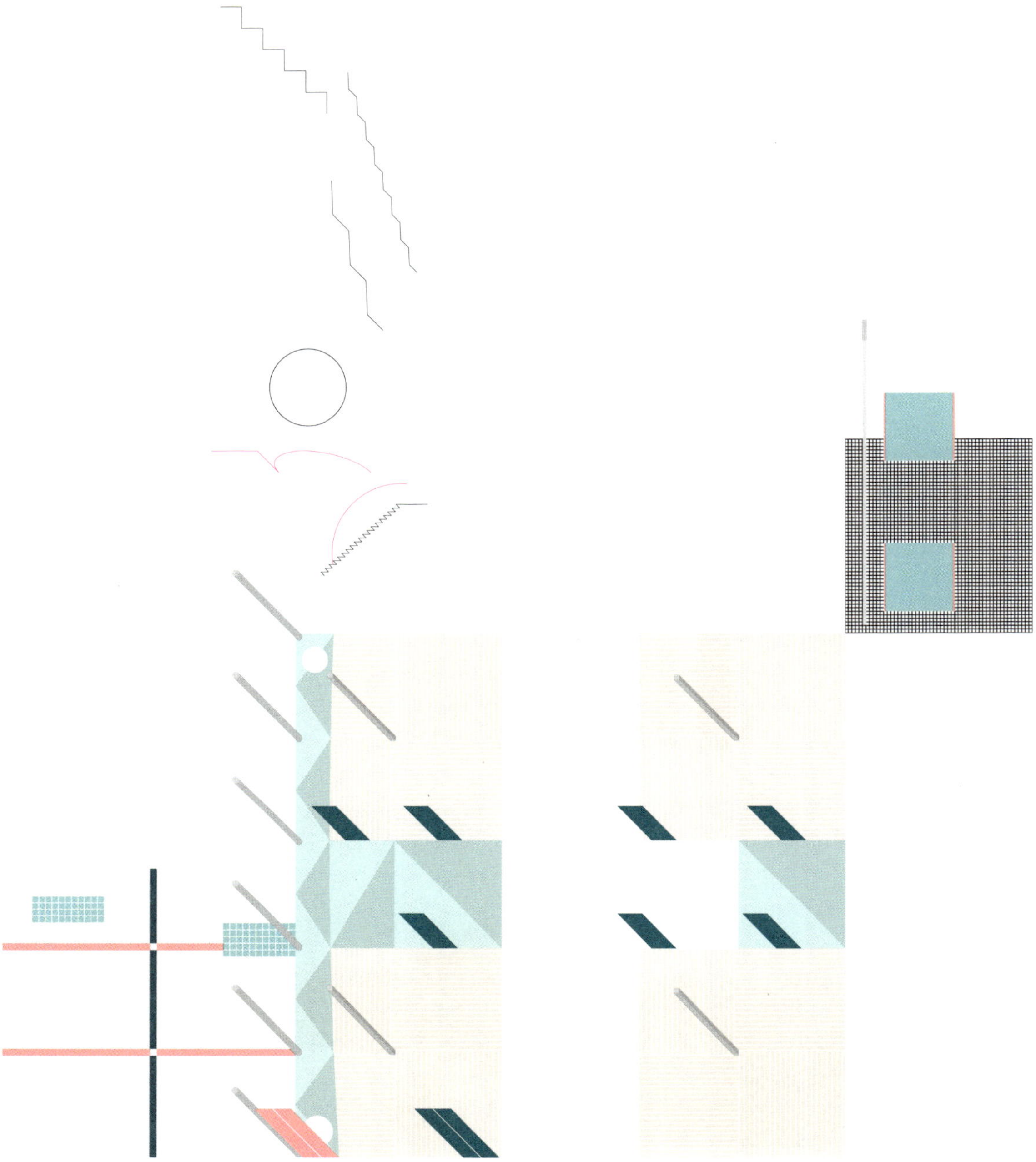

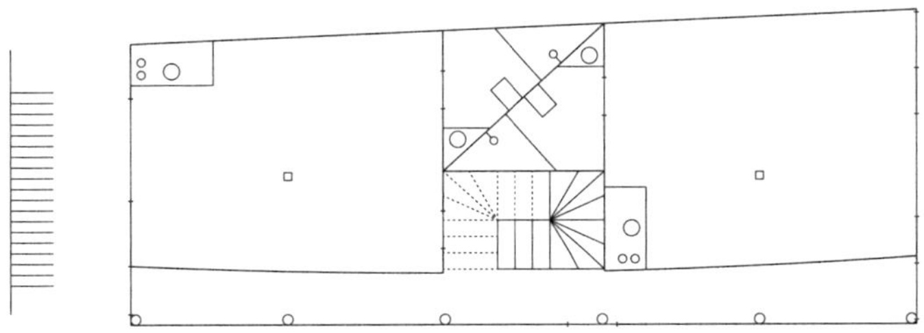

Ground floor

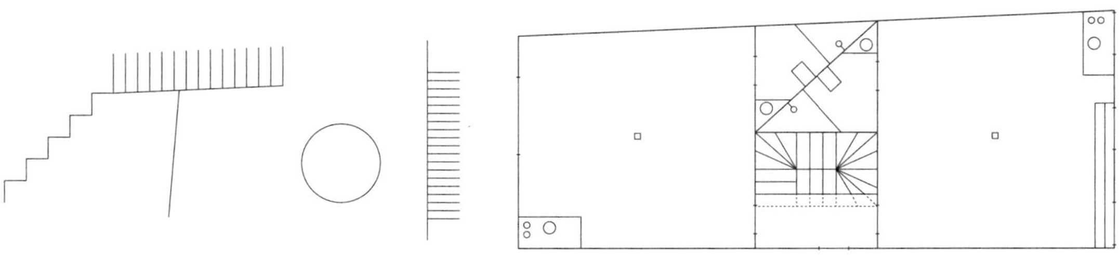

First floor

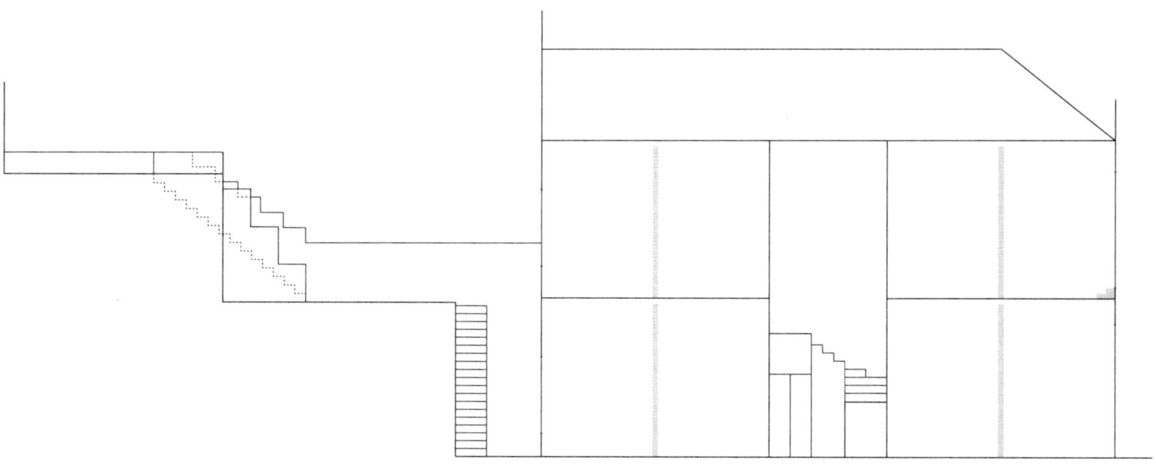

Longitudinal section

House with Four Columns, Porto

House and Atelier, Porto

2017-2018

The old building is hidden in the city center. It has three levels, three entrance doors and a distorted outline. Each floor suggests a different spatial logic but shares the same language, the same materiality and the same set of banal elements.

The ground floor is an open plan atelier connected to the garden. The first floor has a studio apartment with a unique white-and-pink-striped door. The last level is taken up by the biggest apartment, where six rooms are carefully organized around a tall central hall. All the interior spaces are white with a few exposed concrete elements and a couple of exceptional moments. The doors are lacquered in glossy white with exposed plywood frames. The soft chess pattern of the blue terrazzo floor doesn't match the walls and binds all the levels.

The house has only two elevations. The original front façade was unbalanced and slightly curved. It is restructured: the three doors get a strong color, one window disappears, a marble circle is introduced and the tall hat becomes visible from afar. The back façade is rebuilt. The proportion is very different from the front one, taller and narrower. A clear hierarchy reflects the program distribution. It begins with the thin round freestanding column. The pink door contrasts with the large opening and four identical windows suggest a domestic use in the upper levels. The white-painted concrete wall flies above the fragile glazed surface. The circle disturbs its symmetry and finishes the figure.

Living and working in the same building is a delicate convenience. Each level of the building is an independent field of experimentation in which the main common thread is a certain sense of joy.

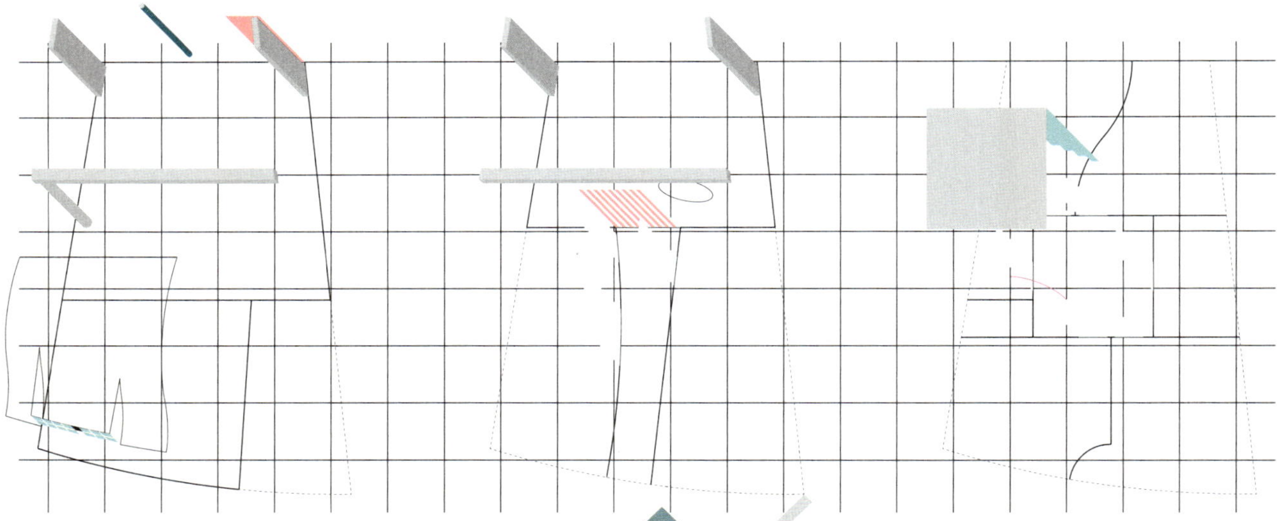

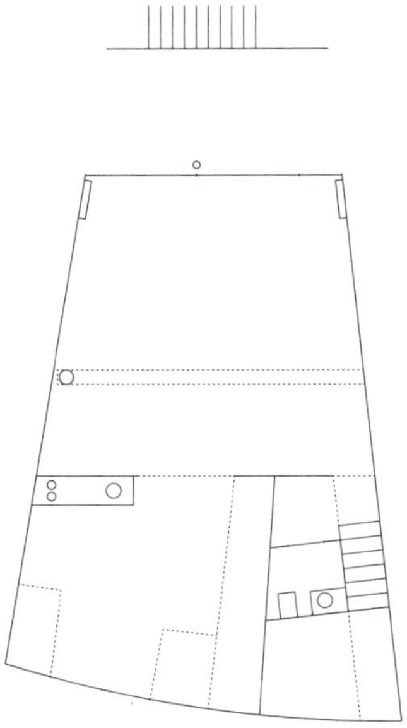

Basement

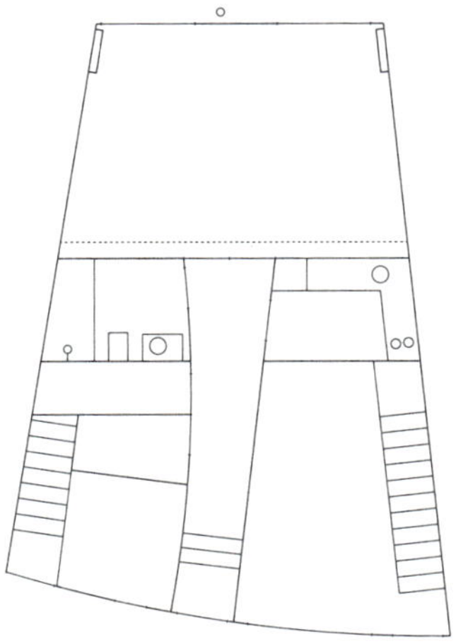

Ground floor

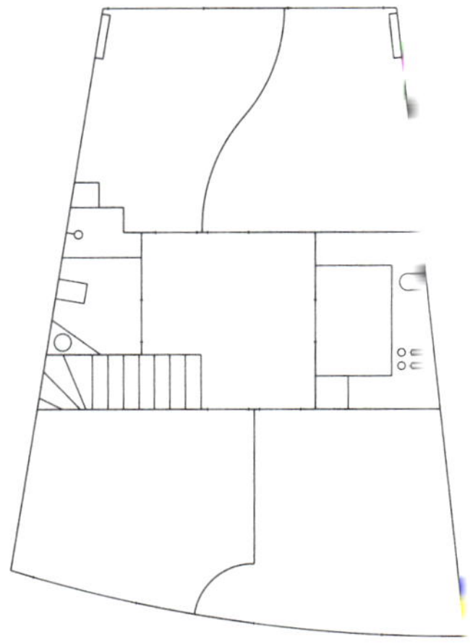

First floor

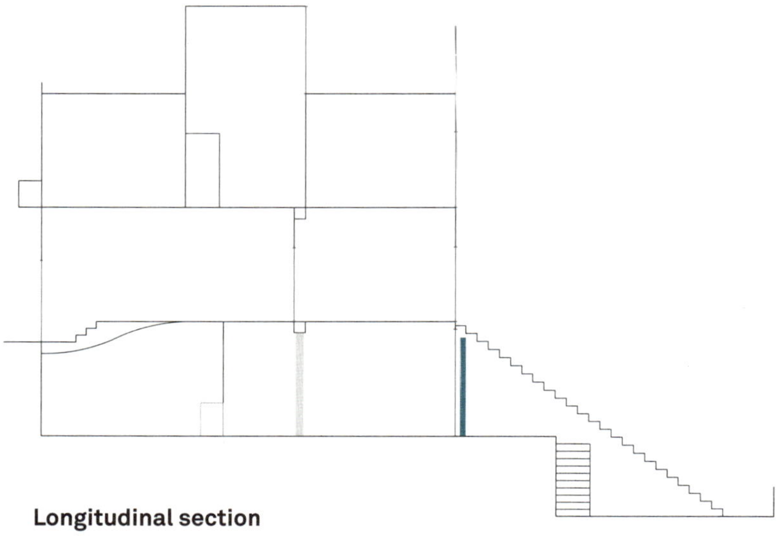

Longitudinal section

Folly for an Art Piece, Porto

2017

A temporary art gallery for an unknown art piece in a sloped garden. The site was remote yet absolute; the brief was vague and open to speculation.

A folly, as the word itself suggests, is an extravagant, frivolous or unreal building, conceived more for artistic expression than for functional reasons. The proposed art gallery was, indeed, all of that. Through a polyphonic repertoire it aimed at being a temple, a temporary construction and a toy, both neoclassical and postmodern.

A misleading rational structure enclosed a cubic volume. The understandable metrics of the wood elements found a mismatch in the proportions of the openings and in the apparently arbitrary colors. A plinth erased the building's relationship with the sloping terrain. Two circles of black marble marked the entrances while a red beam crossed the inner space. Inside, five lounge chairs provided a vague sense of domesticity to the otherwise monumental construction.

The art piece, a short film about contemplation and leisure, managed to dialogue with both the park and the lightheartedness of the architecture. Perhaps the folly was to architectural language what the film was to leisure: a joyful and reflective pastiche... half toy, half temple, half sensible.

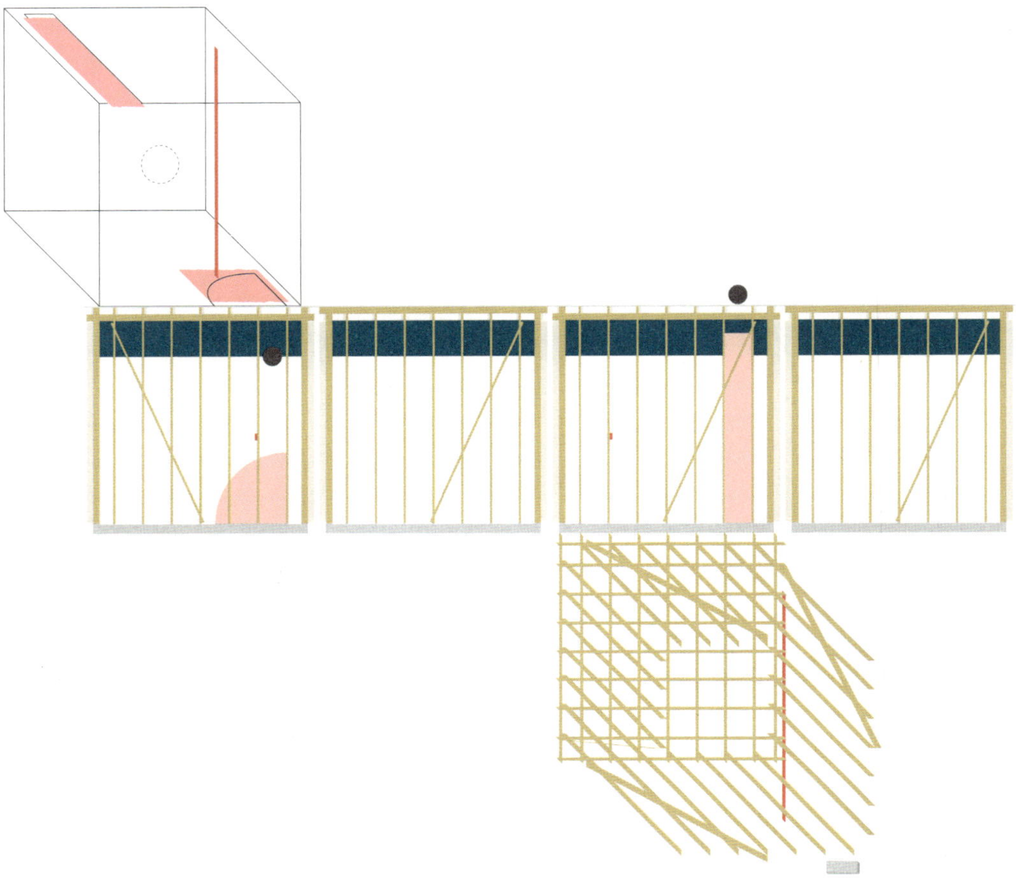

Broken House, Porto

2017-2019

An odd, asymmetrical Art Deco house, nested in the urban fabric, searched for clarity after an erratic succession of renovations and extensions.

The rooms are open to typological diversity, despite the rigid plan repeated in every level. All living spaces revolve around ambiguous rooms, broken in their middle and punctuated by central metallic columns, suggesting a fragmented reading of their otherwise unitary material appearance. The metallic elements function as the only vertical ornament of the domestic spaces, in which the floors are built with three kinds of wood, forming stripes of varying widths, acting as an endless tapestry.

The spiral staircase ties the house together: glossy dark-blue doors, a pre-existing romanticized handrail and a chessboard of different tones of marble make for a cheerful parade.

The Art Deco house is completed with horizontal light yellow stripes facing the street and vertical black and white stripes facing the garden. This language of bands is carried along to both façades as a binding counterforce to the heterogeneity of the project. The house finds a happy coherence in the small incoherences of its architecture. Somehow a new kind of peace is found, fragile and festive.

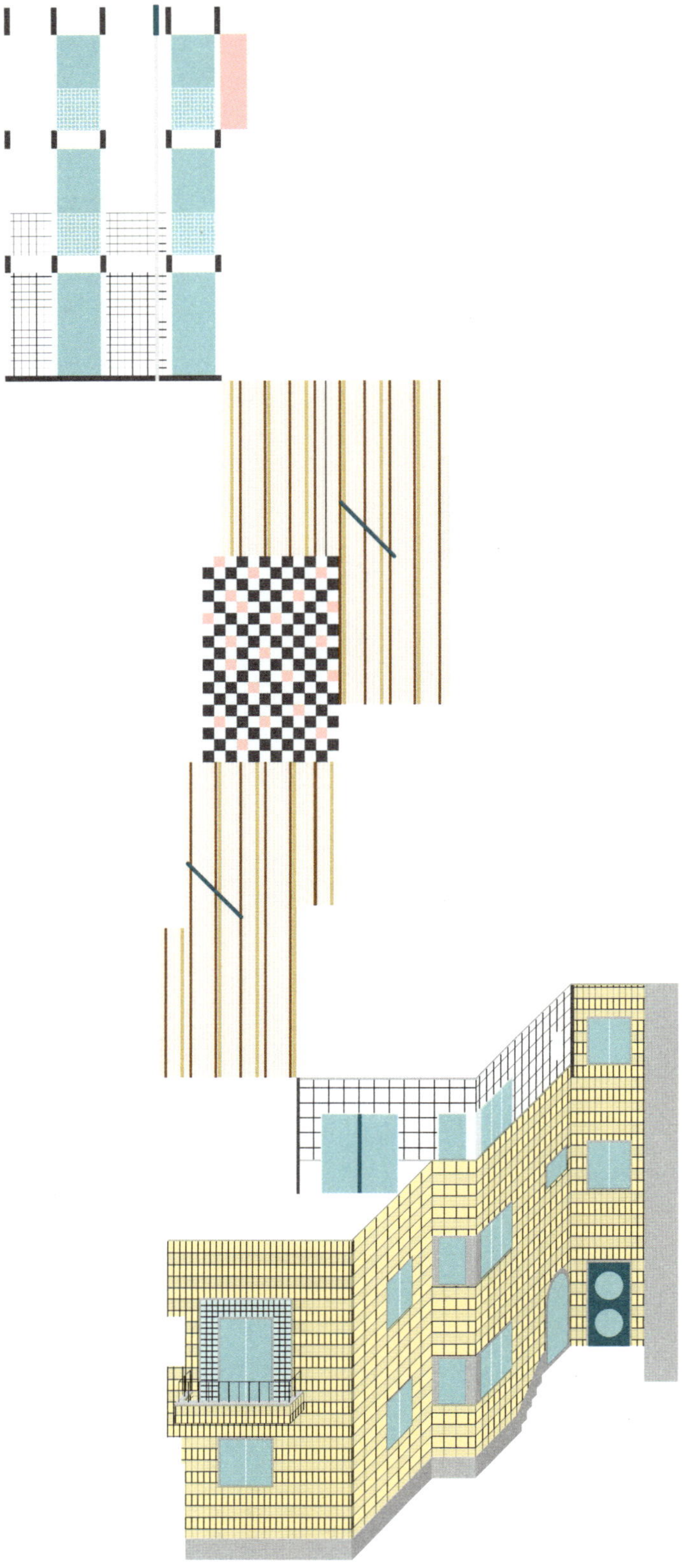

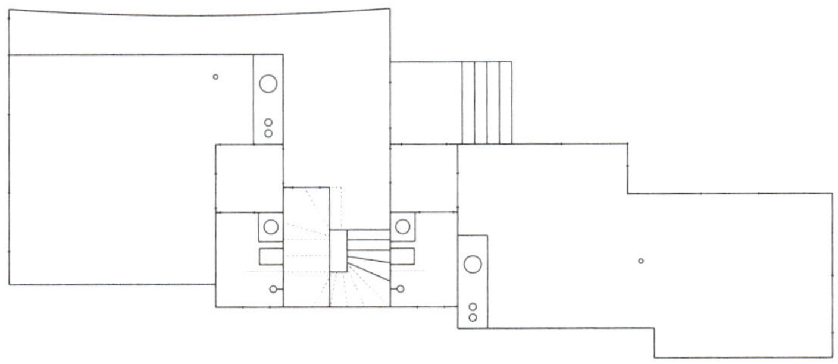

Ground floor

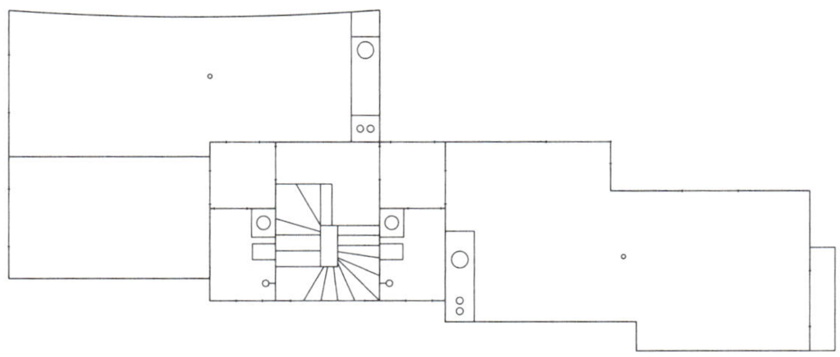

First floor

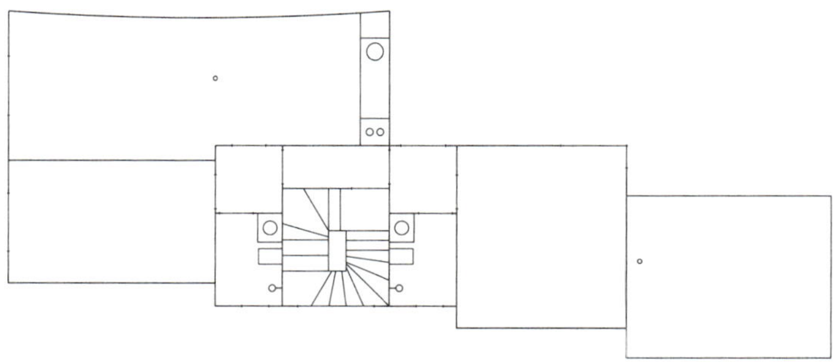

Second floor

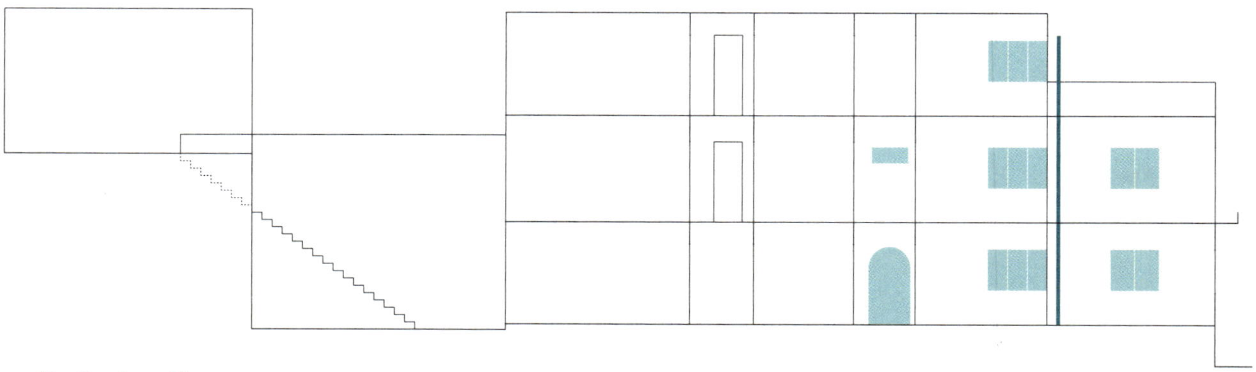

Longitudinal section

House under a Big Roof, Famalicão

2017-

A square plan is deliberately cut, achieving a clear separation between public and private programs. The straightforward simplicity of the living room contrasts with the intricate geometries and reasonable kinks of bedrooms and bathrooms. An erotic duality was proposed.

The materiality of the inside spaces is both gentle and explicit. Thin wooden beams that support the blue ceiling are kept exposed; the wood floors follow different directions and detached doors and cabinetry accent different spatial transitions. The intelligent symmetry of the living room outlines three defined moments for the family: cooking, eating, living. The sloped high ceiling unbalances the symbolic main space.

Floating in a beautiful garden between the neighbors' sheds and fences, the outside expression of the house is solved within a number of carefully placed elements: a blue chimney facing the street, a tall main door suggesting a ceremonial entrance, a proud concrete beam crowning the construction. A set of square windows composes the four white elevations. The generous sloped roof is covered with a playful pattern of traditional ceramic tiles. The figure of the house is detached from the ground with a line of black and white tiles, softly dissociating itself from the soil it occupies.

The clients requested a house that "looked like a house"; the project tackled the definition of "houseness." The concise vocabulary and the precise grammar of the project outline some sort of "challenged vernacular"; an architecture of familiarity and confusion.

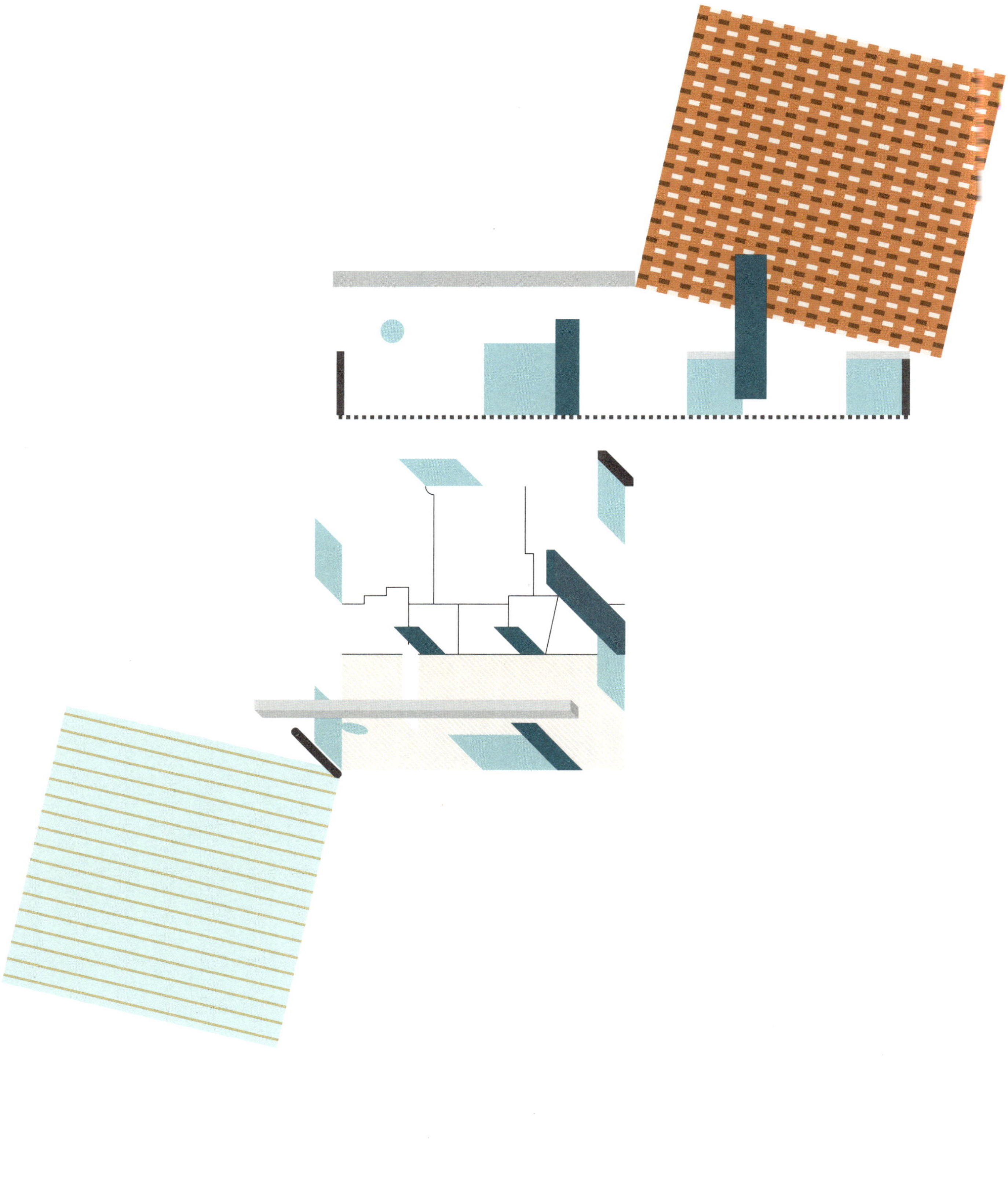

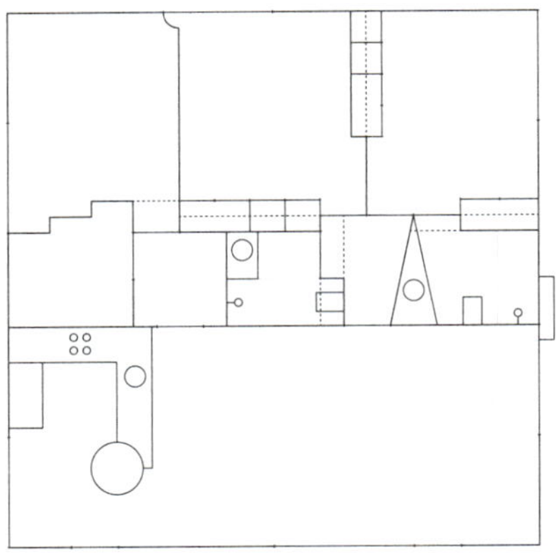

Ground floor

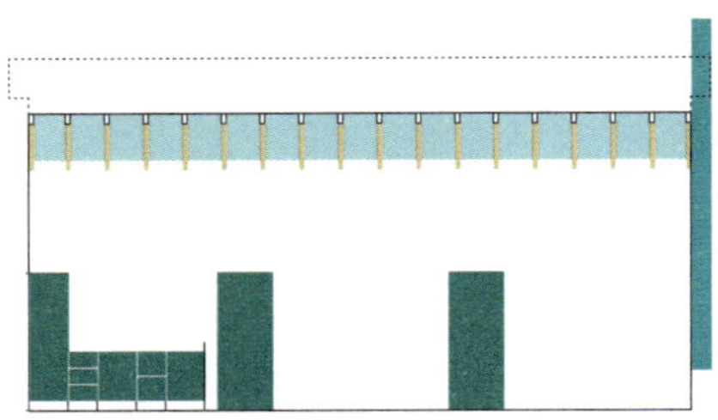

Longitudinal section

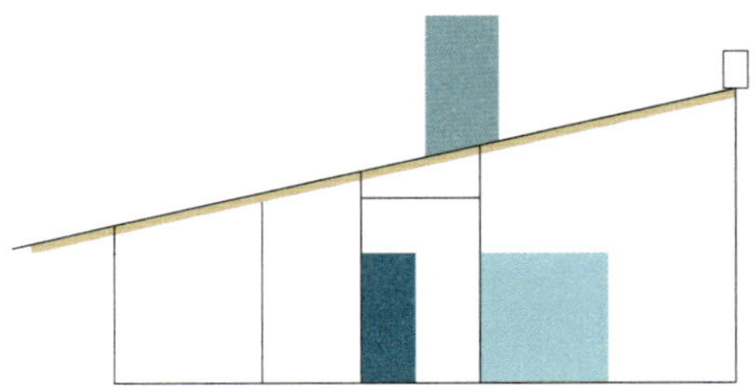

Cross-section

Six Houses and a Garden, Porto

2017-2019

Two buildings with a similar appearance, one very long and another very short. Six houses —four identical and two exceptional—around one common garden, hidden inside a city block. One architecture tying the fragmented reality.

The composition of each inner space combines orthogonal, diagonal and curved lines. The slightly distorted perimeter of the rooms sets the frames; the main spaces come from a subtraction of conflicting surfaces that comprise secondary programs. The thin metal poles bring in vertical tension; the round openings connect uneven programs. Acting within a very small volume, this combination of ambivalent geometries achieves unconventional living spaces.

The materiality of the awkward interiors follows their complexity. Walls are merely white, the horizontal slabs are abrupt concrete, the floors display polished blue marble and the tilted ceiling is painted in pink. Wooden doors, exaggerated handles and hints of pink marble accompany this game of surfaces.

On the outside, the houses define a continuous colonnade framing a collective garden where it becomes impossible to understand where each houses begins or ends. The façade is an overlap of several rhythmic rows—the thin metal columns, the striped blue doors, the black boxy skylights. The roof is made of two layers: a pink wavy plane is attached below the metal sheets, emphasizing the thinness of the surface. All around, the most honest and beautiful urban scenario defines the idyllic background for such an architectural exercise.

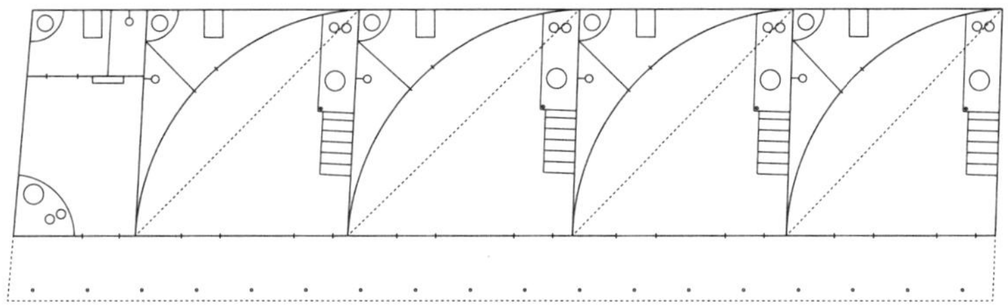

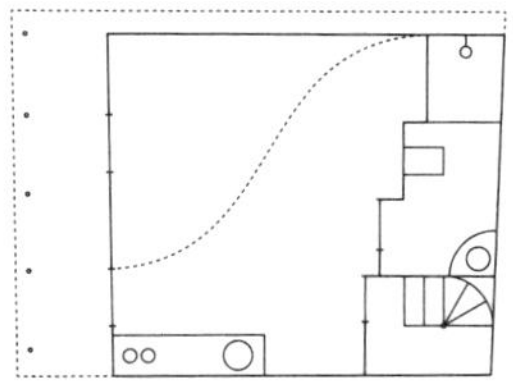

Ground floor

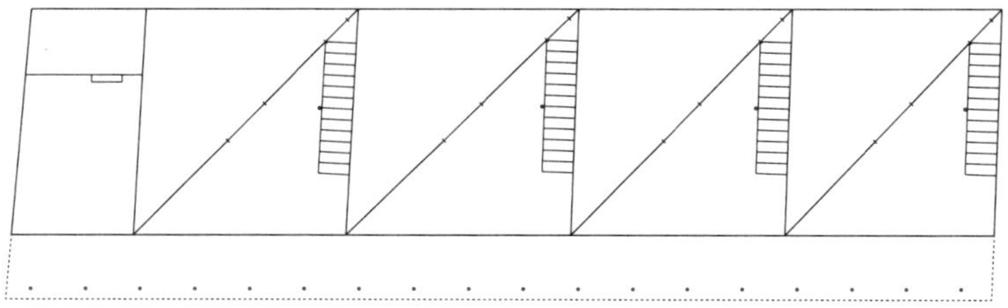

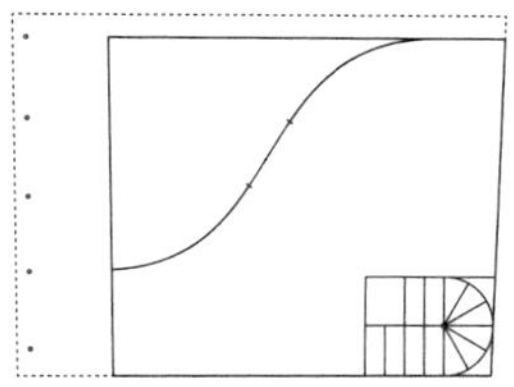

First floor

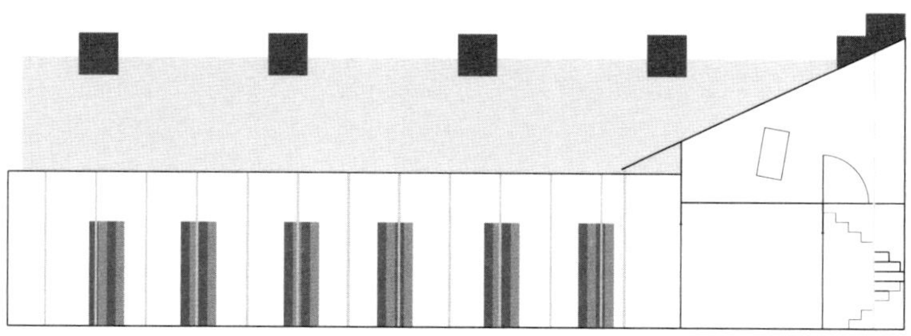

Cross-section

Suspended House, Porto

2017-

In an artery connecting the city center to its suburbs, where individual houses are being demolished daily to make way for bigger housing developments, conceiving a new individual house is a delicate task. The façades of the project stemmed from a rough conjugation of both building types, sitting in a fragile ambiguity. A rational order following the logic of the plans is superimposed with a set of seemingly inordinate elements: row windows, erratic marble frontons, seemingly arbitrary drainpipes and pink marble discs unbalancing the composition. The house is an exercise on uniqueness as much as it is an exercise on banality.

The interior follows similar policies. An off-centered column functions as a hinge and divides each level into four equivalent quadrants. There are three levels, with street access on the middle one. Fixed or flexible programs uniformly occupy these quadrants, leaving the use to the user. The house is a static frame for the changing dynamics of life. Its central column is a condensing, symbolical element, a substratum of these dynamics. Its shape is arbitrary and exuberant, providing distinct perspectives to each room. A collection of blue doors interconnects different rooms and adorns the column like superhero capes.

On the lower level, undivided and open to the garden, the column levitates a few centimeters from the ground. The floor under it is therefore easy to clean, and the fragility of the entire structure is revealed. A house is always a mental construct before being anything else.

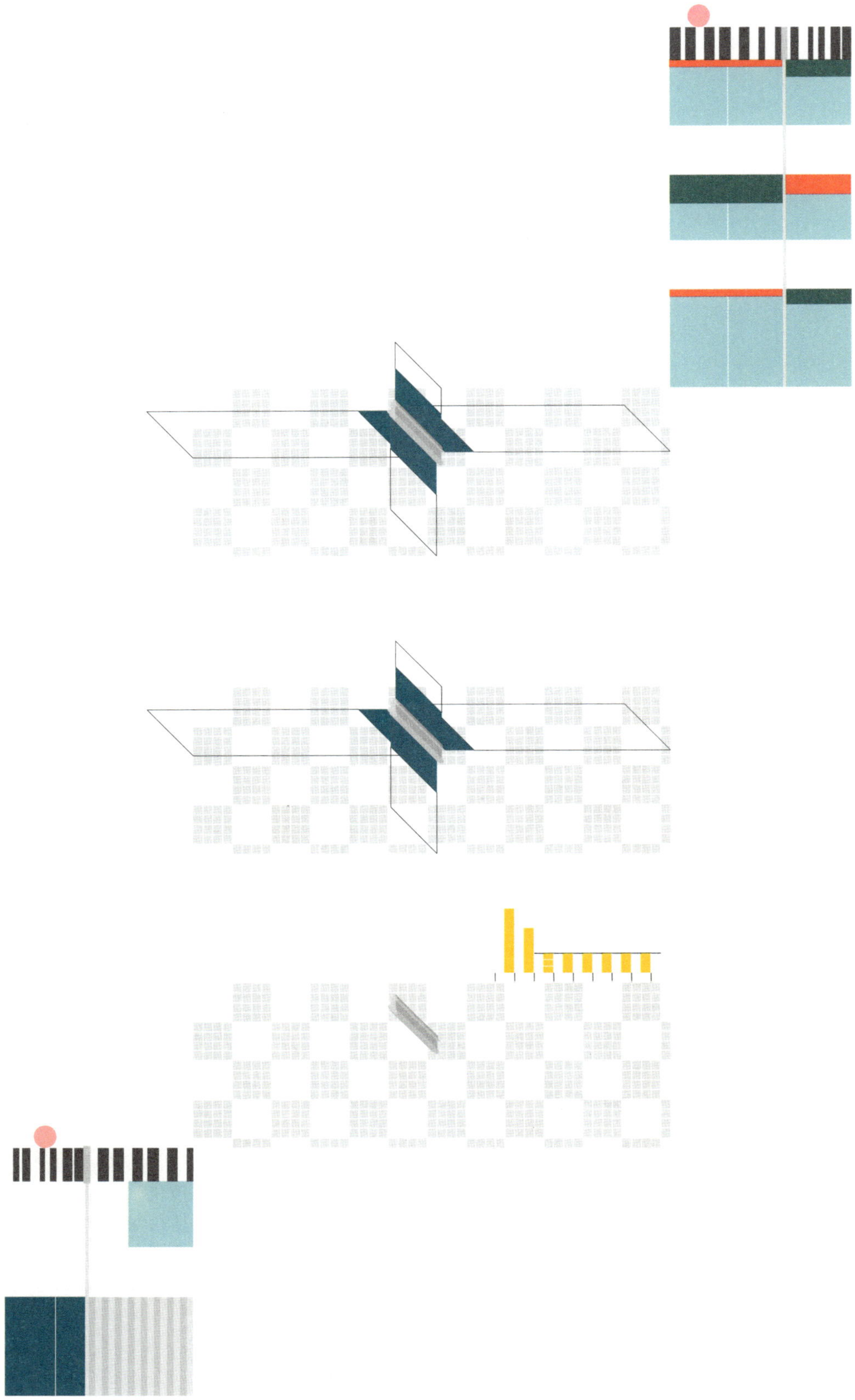

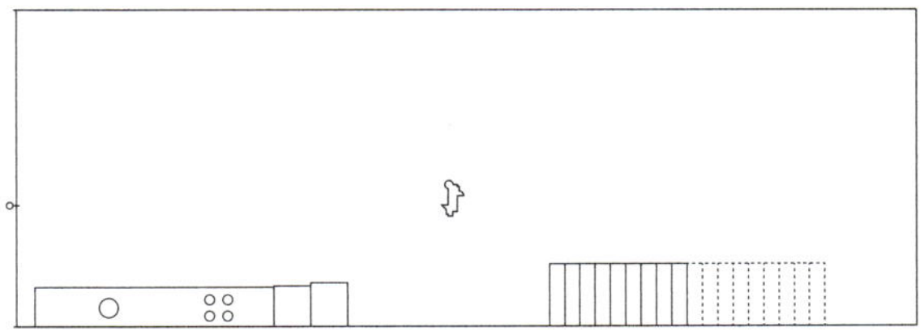

Ground floor

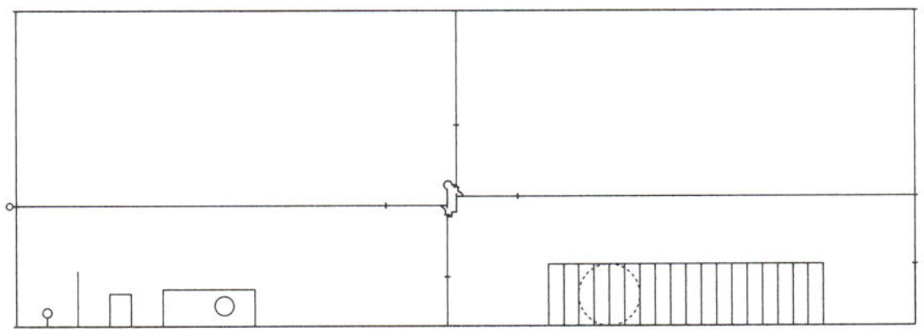

First floor

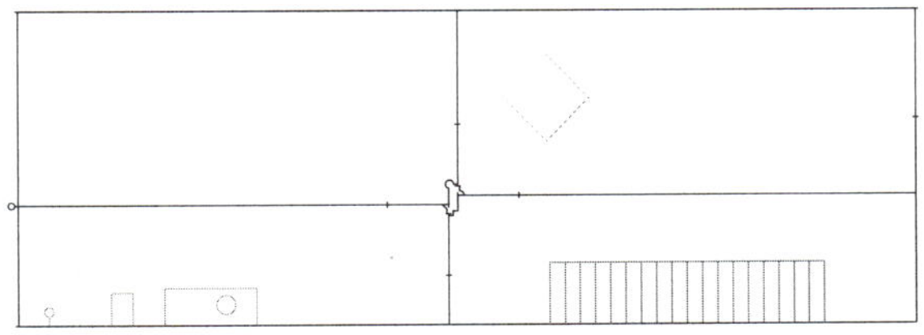

Second floor

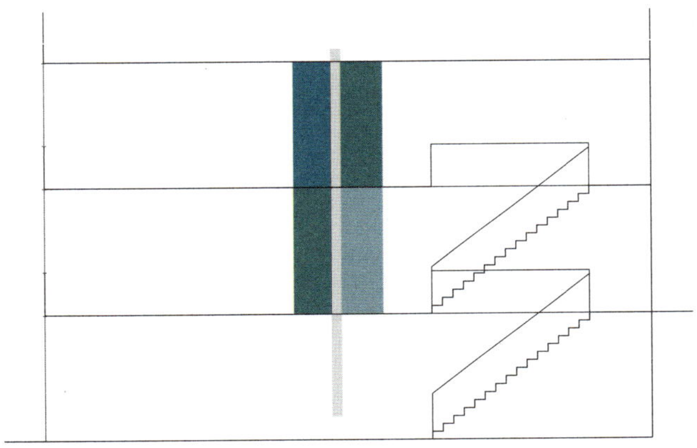

Longitudinal section

Small House with a Monumental Shower, Amarante

2017-2018

Conceiving a house within a very old and small granite shack, with a slightly distorted plan and a prominent sloped roof, at the edge of a beautiful garden.

Each level is a single space with a delicate spiral staircase connecting both floors. Relating to the surrounding gardens, the living area occupies the ground floor; the bedroom fits under the sloped roof, facing the views.

The only added volume is an exuberant tower bluntly attached to the main volume. The new object is a superimposed element that fits a small bathroom downstairs and a strikingly tall shower above. The interior has its complexities and circumstances. A curved wall on the first floor is introduced to hold both pieces together, hide technical pipes and some storage, as well as to cause a subtle distortion of the bedroom. The inside spaces are defined with a simple palette of materials—white walls, striped wooden floors, fractions of white marble and mint-green carpentries. A nice house to live in.

From the outside, the ambiguous pattern of white and pink triangles makes an obvious contrast between the two actors. The outward expression is dominated by this exuberant pattern and the new thin metal roof flying above the granite piece. The texture of the granite walls is kept and all the doors and window frames are refreshed with color.

The tall tower is standing in paradoxical independence, refusing to be serious, making a courageous formal statement. A monumental object for a non-monumental program.

Apartment on a Mint Floor, Porto

2018-2019

Located on the *piano nobile* of a modernist housing block, the apartment faced a reclaimed terrace; the interiors were reconfigured with little empathy towards the original plan.

A convoluted main space, on the edge of fragmentation, spans from façade to façade. It incorporates a living and dining area, an almost separate kitchen and the possibility of an additional bedroom. The main bedroom and both bathrooms are concealed behind a simple circular wall. The amount of walls is kept to a minimum; their layout is strategic.

The project operates through a set of gentle oppositions between existing and added elements. The circular wall counteracts the complexity of the vertical circulations of the building. The humble interior finishes underline the presence of the various fixtures and structural elements. Monumental wood doors suggest different degrees of privacy and a patterned kitchen lazes in the abundant sunlight.

The new façade facing the terrace, generously open, hints at the modernism of the street façade and in doing so finds a contrast with its direct context. The mint-green floor firmly binds all spaces together despite the irresolute hierarchy of the plan.

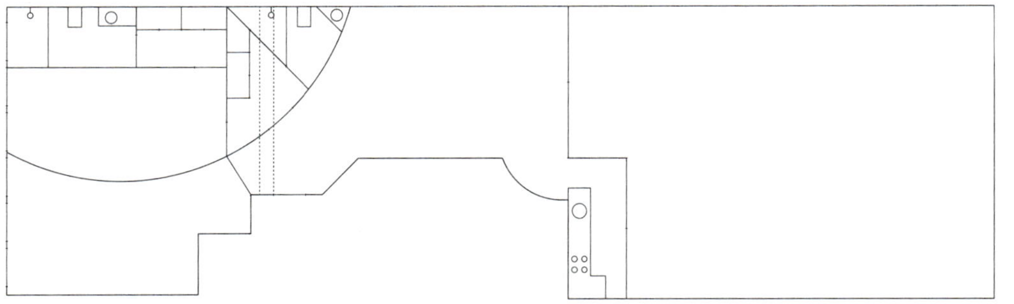

First floor

Longitudinal section

CCCP

House along a Wall, Porto

2018

The program for a former garage of a housing block was kept in limbo: maybe an apartment, a shop, a cafe or an art gallery.

A freely curved wall solves the existing spatial inconsistencies and creates one long continuous room connecting the street with the garden. The main living area and a set of potential secondary programs are separated by the wavy white surface and light flows freely through the living gallery.

The old metal gate is replaced with a set of strict hammered glass panels. A circle of black marble, which is both a door handle and a mailbox, marks the entrance and addresses the city.

The back façade is completely open, defining a composition of isolated elements: a sliding window, a blue concrete freestanding column, a final circle of black marble. The backyard has a seamless perimeter of rough white walls, a terrace and a calm garden.

The materiality of the project is light and abstract. The space is defined through the geometry of the terrazzo floor pattern and a number of carefully placed elements. The white-blue triangulated terrazzo pattern follows the curved wall, allowing the living area to maintain a certain unity and coherence. The flying kitchen counter, three green doors and the circular opening imply possible usages while suggesting also a certain complexity. The garage, that could still work as such, becomes an uncertain spatial experience.

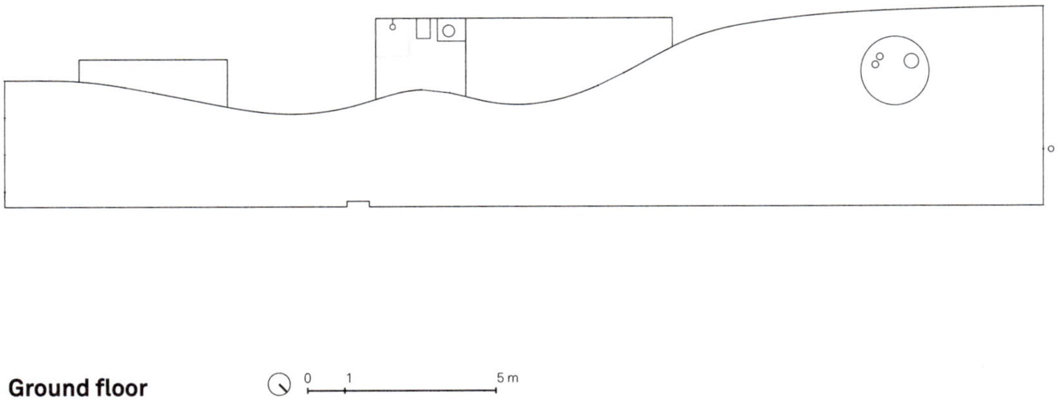

Ground floor

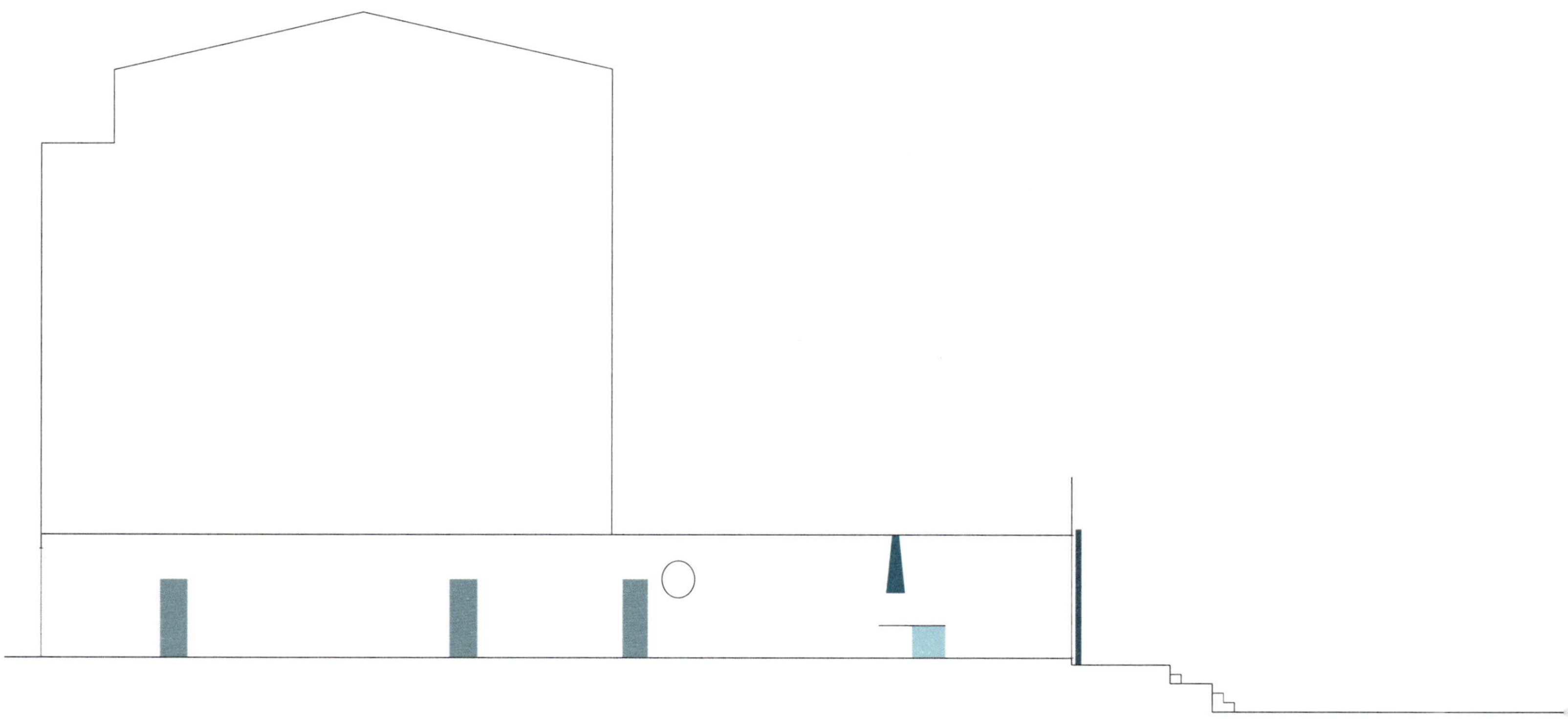

Longitudinal section

Uneven House, Porto

2018-2019

A ground-floor shop and its basement were to be converted into an apartment. An extension at the back was demolished to provide a garden, from which the new house would become the plinth to a cheerless 1960s housing block.

Both levels are conceived as a main room spanning the two façades. The longitudinal spaces are defined by a straight white wall on one side and a composite wall opposite (comprising three massive plywood doors to the secondary programs). While the walls play their own formal game, the position of the doors and the finishes remain the same on both levels.

The inner logic also dictates the façade on the garden side, which acts as if the house was only one very tall level. In fact, both levels have floor-to-ceiling glass openings towards the outside, thanks to a new staircase dug in front of the garden.

As the loadbearing structure of the building goes through the project, its visual presence is challenged by claddings of marble and mirrors. The glorious stone pattern extends outside as a black-and-white striped frieze marking the perimeter of the garden, a grand horizontal window framing the context.

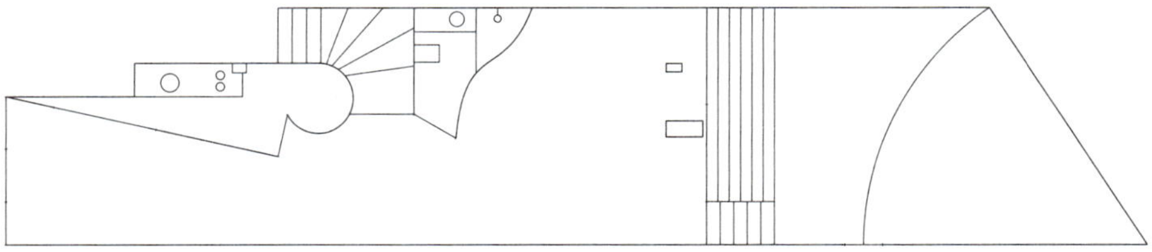

Ground floor

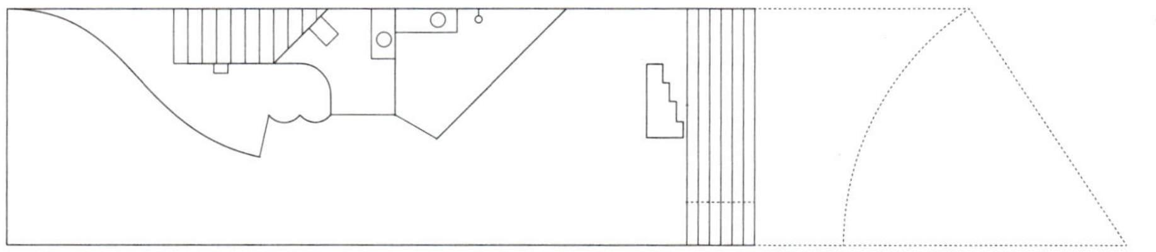

Basement

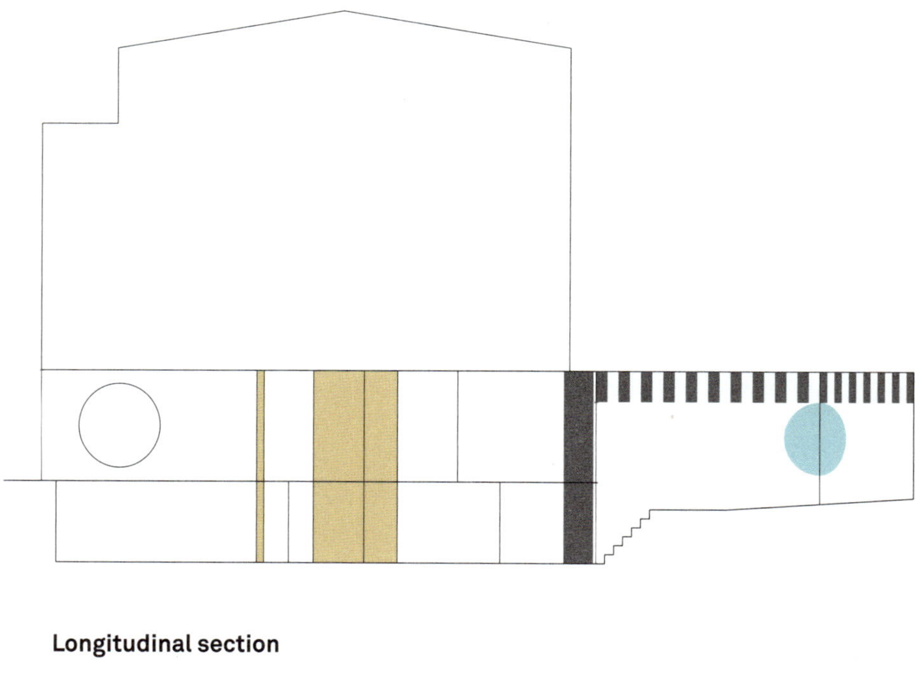

Longitudinal section

Folly for Sun and Sound, Brussels

2019

The structure doesn't exactly decide between being a stage, a room or a plaza. It is made of a series of plateaus and four façades with distinct characters. The overall volume recalls the nearby barracks but its language has nothing military about it.

Essentially made of local wood, a careful use of paint clarifies the reading of the architectural elements. The coherence of the project is proudly loose and open to interpretation. Green and white plywood tiles become feathers towards the outside, horizontal stripes on the inside. A metal roof welcomes guests in, protects the stage, and provides support for two disco balls. One of the short façades looks like a rising moon, the other recalls a white cat lying in the sun.

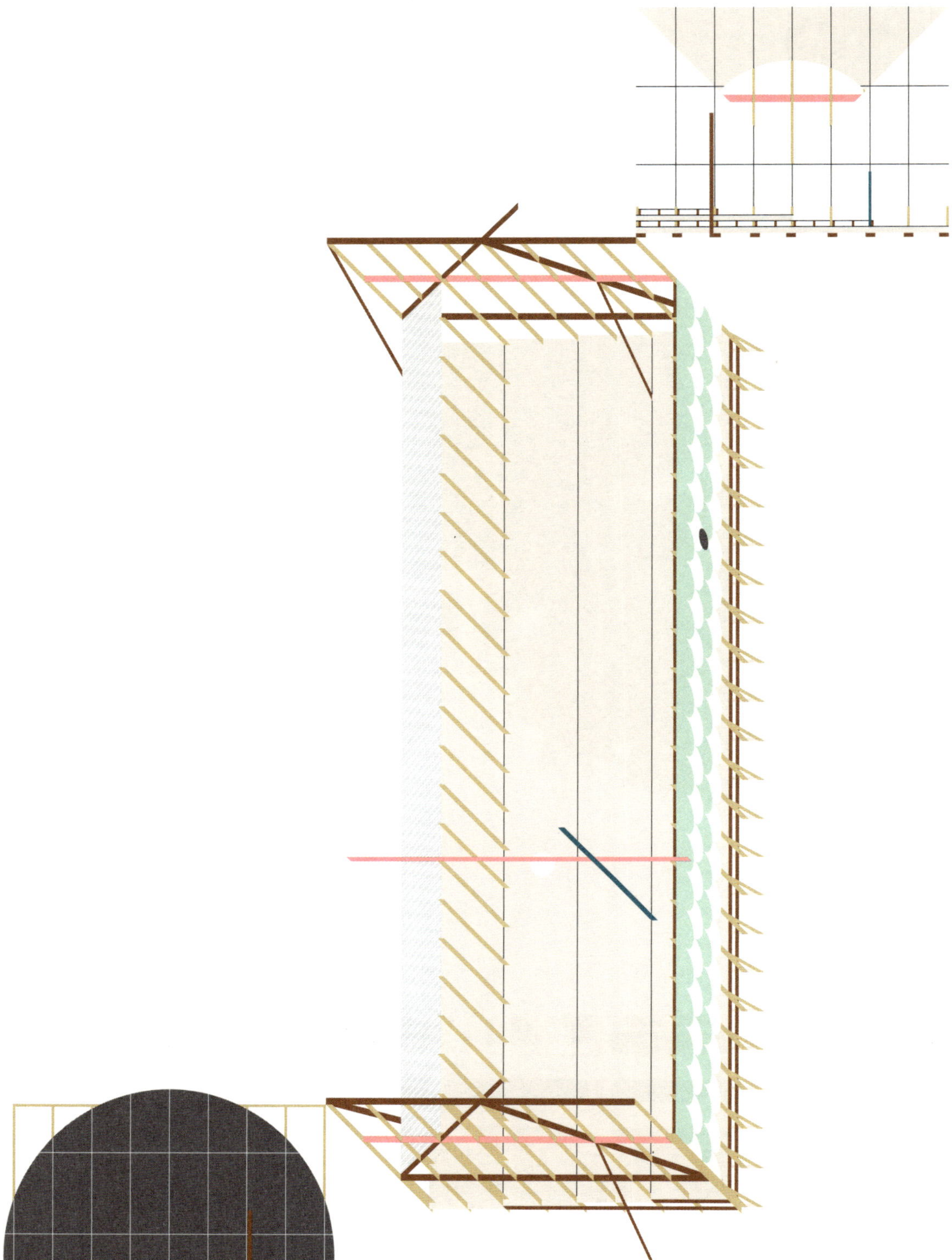

Folly for Sun and Sound, Brussels

Folly for Sun and Sound, Brussels

Credits

House for Three Generations

Location Marco de Canaveses, Portugal
Architects fala (Filipe Magalhães, Ana Luisa Soares, Ahmed Belkhodja)
Collaborators Julia Andreychenko, Camelia Petre, Paulo Sousa
Design and construction years 2015-
Surface area 180 m²
Contractor ASV lda
Photography fala, Ricardo Loureiro

House in Paraíso

Location Porto, Portugal
Architects fala (Filipe Magalhães, Ana Luisa Soares, Ahmed Belkhodja)
Collaborators Rute Peixoto, Lera Samovich, Paulo Sousa
Design and construction years 2016-2017
Landscape architect Pomo
Surface area 150 m²
Contractor Engilaco lda
Photography Ricardo Loureiro

Reasonable Housing

Location Penafiel, Portugal
Architects fala (Filipe Magalhães, Ana Luisa Soares, Ahmed Belkhodja)
Collaborators Julia Andreychenko, Rute Peixoto, Lera Samovich, Paulo Sousa
Design and construction years 2016-2018
Landscape architect Pomo
Surface area 680 m²
Contractor Ruce lda
Photography Ricardo Loureiro

House in Fontaínhas

Location Porto, Portugal
Architects fala (Filipe Magalhães, Ana Luisa Soares, Ahmed Belkhodja)
Collaborators Ana Lima, Rute Peixoto, Lera Samovich, Elisa Sassi, Paulo Sousa
Design and construction years 2016-2019
Landscape architect Pomo
Surface area 200 m²
Contractor Civiflanco lda
Photography Ricardo Loureiro

House with a Curved Wall

Location Porto, Portugal
Architects fala (Filipe Magalhães, Ana Luisa Soares, Ahmed Belkhodja)
Collaborators Julia Andreychenko, Rute Peixoto, Lera Samovich, Elisa Sassi, Paulo Sousa
Design and construction years 2016-2017
Landscape architect Pomo
Surface area 95 m²
Contractor Maxrenova lda
Photography Ricardo Loureiro

House with Four Columns

Location Porto, Portugal
Architects fala (Filipe Magalhães, Ana Luisa Soares, Ahmed Belkhodja)
Collaborators Rute Peixoto, Lera Samovich, Elisa Sassi, Joana Sendas, Paulo Sousa
Design and construction years 2016-2018
Landscape architect Pomo
Surface area 220 m²
Contractor Engilaco lda
Photography Ricardo Loureiro

House and Atelier

Location Porto, Portugal
Architects fala (Filipe Magalhães, Ana Luisa Soares, Ahmed Belkhodja)
Collaborators Costanza Favero, Ana Lima, Rute Peixoto, Lera Samovich, Elisa Sassi, Joana Sendas, Paulo Sousa
Design and construction years 2017-2018
Landscape architect Pomo
Surface area 250 m²
Contractor Engilaco lda
Photography Ricardo Loureiro

Folly for an Art Piece

Location Fundação de Serralves, Porto, Portugal
Architects fala (Filipe Magalhães, Ana Luisa Soares, Ahmed Belkhodja)
Collaborators Rute Peixoto, Lera Samovich, Elisa Sassi, Paulo Sousa
Design and construction year 2017
Surface area 30 m²
Client Fundação de Serralves, São Paulo Biennial
Contractor JST lda
Photography Ricardo Loureiro

Broken House

Location Porto, Portugal
Architects fala (Filipe Magalhães, Ana Luisa Soares, Ahmed Belkhodja)
Collaborators Elisa Sassi, Joana Sendas, Paulo Sousa
Design and construction years 2017-2019
Landscape architect Pomo
Surface area 260 m²
Contractor Maxrenova lda
Photography Ricardo Loureiro

House under a Big Roof

Location Famalicão, Portugal
Architects fala (Filipe Magalhães, Ana Luisa Soares, Ahmed Belkhodja)
Collaborators Lera Samovich, Paulo Sousa
Design and construction years 2017-
Surface area 115 m²
Contractor ASV lda, Joph lda
Photography Ricardo Loureiro

Six Houses and a Garden

Location Porto, Portugal
Architects fala (Filipe Magalhães, Ana Luisa Soares, Ahmed Belkhodja)
Collaborators Rute Peixoto, Lera Samovich, Paulo Sousa
Design and construction years 2017-2019
Landscape architect Pomo
Surface area 190 m²
Contractor Civiflanco lda
Photography Ricardo Loureiro

Suspended House

Location Porto, Portugal
Architects fala (Filipe Magalhães, Ana Luisa Soares, Ahmed Belkhodja)
Collaborators Costanza Favero, Ana Lima, Lera Samovich, Joana Sendas, Paulo Sousa
Design and construction years 2017-
Surface area 270 m²
Contractor JST lda
Photography fala

Small House with a Monumental Shower

Location Amarante, Portugal
Architects fala (Filipe Magalhães, Ana Luisa Soares, Ahmed Belkhodja)
Collaborators Costanza Favero, Ana Lima, Joana Sendas, Paulo Sousa
Design and construction years 2017-2018
Surface area 38 m²
Contractor Ruce lda
Photography Ricardo Loureiro

Apartment on a Mint Floor

Location Porto, Portugal
Architects fala (Filipe Magalhães, Ana Luisa Soares, Ahmed Belkhodja)
Collaborators Costanza Favero, Joana Sendas, Paulo Sousa
Design and construction years 2018-2019
Surface area 100 m²
Contractor Engilaco lda
Photography Ricardo Loureiro

House along a Wall

Location Porto, Portugal
Architects fala (Filipe Magalhães, Ana Luisa Soares, Ahmed Belkhodja)
Collaborators Costanza Favero, Ana Lima, Joana Sendas, Paulo Sousa
Design and construction year 2018
Landscape architect Pomo
Surface area 150 m²
Contractor Civiflanco lda
Photography Ricardo Loureiro

Uneven House

Location Porto, Portugal
Architects fala (Filipe Magalhães, Ana Luisa Soares, Ahmed Belkhodja)
Collaborators Costanza Favero, Paulo Sousa
Design and construction years 2018-2019
Landscape architect Pomo
Surface area 150 m²
Contractor Civiflanco lda
Photography Ricardo Loureiro

Folly for Sun and Sound

Location Brussels, Belgium
Architects fala (Filipe Magalhães, Ana Luisa Soares, Ahmed Belkhodja)
Collaborators Beatriz Branco, Lera Samovich, Paulo Sousa
Design and construction year 2019
Surface area 284 m²
Client Horst Arts & Music Festival
Photography fala

NEXUS

Gloriously Repeating

fala

Maybe because we are naïve, we thought that what we had learned in a few years was enough to run a practice. Architecture, immediately. The beginning of a long-term commitment, an endless and daily production, as if taking any time to step back would seize up the machine. We threw ourselves in the ocean to learn how to swim, with no clients and little funds, but with enthusiasm and a bookshelf. Today our belief is that the most challenging and politically charged step an architect can take is to conceive a practice.

As sentimental as this may sound, it is a matter of overriding passion. fala is a combination of curiosity, ambitious youth, cynical naïveté, lack of seriousness, a simple fascination for architecture and our awkward humor. A humor that is used to say something serious.

A group of people, not exactly cohesive, that gather for a few hours every day in a small white building in Porto. Some of us actually live on the two floors above the atelier, blurring even further the boundaries between private life and work space. All of us, except Harry, use the same tools and work on all projects and phases. Harry has different responsibilities because he's a cat. The atmosphere is both light and communal. We have crushes on rooms, façades and columns. We laugh at what we do, talk about buildings like people and sometimes give them surnames. There is the assumed freedom of an office that is still in its formative years.

All forms of gravity are despised but a few things are taken seriously: line thicknesses and tea-making. But also certain names that are repeated like mantras; heroes that we adore but never truly understand. They are most often architects and they come from all around the globe: Kazuo Shinohara, Erik Gunnar Asplund, Álvaro Siza, Peter Märkli, Ellsworth Kelly, Itsuko Hasegawa, Luigi Ghirri, Robert Venturi, Mario Botta… The list is long but not endless and sometimes a new name shyly emerges. To a certain extent the practice could be described as a rather cute cult devoted to them. We are geeks and architecture fans before being architects. We might spend months looking for one of their buildings on online maps, just for the raw satisfaction of knowing it still stands in its more or less original form. In a few lucky instances we might get to knock at the door one day. Sometimes that leads to a memorable visit but most often we get chased away by the owners. Irrational perhaps, but not entirely vain. The works of these heroes are our only wealth and compass. The belief is that anything from the past that is good to the eyes of today is good enough to work from and that adoration is a good antidote to hubris. As a matter of fact, most of these people were or are still looking at precedents themselves.

Our love is unrequited but it is still part of an eco-system: this might well be another aspect of our naïveté. We refuse to claim anything architectural as ours, and we value misunderstandings. The entire history of architecture could well be understood as a series of failed interpretations, productive mistakes in translation. Björk once said of a famous architect that he "felt oppressed by the oblivious people who are not part of the smart, sophisticated game where everything becomes a quotation from something else."[1] We feel nicely oppressed too, but perhaps this is the necessary discomfort of the architect. As architecture is a smart, sophisticated game where everything becomes a quotation from something else. We should underline here: "becomes," not "is." Because it is a form of knowledge that isn't static. Architecture is a process.

The multiplicity of our guiding heroes translates into unexpected collisions and correspondences, dreamed matches, scenarios for which we act as conductors or vessels. How would a collaboration between Josef Frank and Hiromi Fujii turn out? What if it happened here and now? And what if it was the renovation of an ordinary Portuguese house? More importantly, how would it be perceived? How could one make sure that certain motifs are still relevant? Should one try to be sure of anything? We're not.

1 — Björk about Rem Koolhaas, unpublished interview by Alex Ross for *The New Yorker*, New York, 2004.

Our only insurance is an incremental method in which ideas are tested one by one, project after project, almost as in scientific research. Each found answer opens an array of new questions. And as in the sciences, each new question might ultimately challenge the models one started from. Elements appear almost by accident. A plan principle, a structural principle, a certain type of stripe, a vibrant color, the exuberant shape of a kitchen hood, white walls, easy colors that emerge in slight disorder, wrong angles, curved walls and columns that hold nothing, grids of various kinds, frivolous or rigorous geometries… Each element might become an obsession in a series of projects, then evolve into one possibility among many in the following ones, while newer ones begin their process of digestion. Certain elements may also gradually disappear, or make a comeback. "We haven't drawn a triangular bathroom in quite a while." We look at these waves, study them, but avoid forcing anything. To a certain extent the elements have a life of their own.

We are both spectators and taxonomists in a constant process of cataloguing and surveying each project like an archipelago and all the projects together like a bigger one. All the decisions in all the projects are connected; ideas and forms travel between different designs. The collection of strategies and elements, borrowed from precedents, becomes an architectural vocabulary, a landscape of tropes. They play the same game of order, symmetry and repetition, introduce shifts, mistakes and exceptions. Projects and tropes are seen at the same level, two dimensions of one cartography that helps us understand what we do. One of the most notable results is that each project is a fragmented intervention at heart. "Each of us is many things."[2] All projects are novelties to some degree; furthermore they are all mixtures of the exaggerated, the boring, the naïve, etc. In this context fragility is an existential necessity but also a matter of hope. Each project is the crystallization of a set of ideas at a given moment, but a fragile project welcomes whatever comes after its completion and doesn't need to diminish what precedes it. In the strictest sense of the word, it is inclusive. Violently vivid, but inclusive. It looks outward.

All representation techniques are conscious attempts to flatten this variety, to make it controllable. Collages, single line drawings, exploded or unfolded axonometrics, sketches on top of sketches, collections of low-resolution renderings, photographs, execution drawings and partial drawings, drawings that don't even have a name… The list is endless and they are all necessary, even if not all are meant to be shown. A vigorous visual discourse, images that are charged with meaning.

The practice of building and the practice of drawing run parallel to each other and their trajectories inform each other. A mode of representation that wouldn't have an impact on the way one conceives and builds would be futile. The way we build is a consequence of the way we draw. Making all images in the same format isn't only a sign of our manic obsessions. It is also a first step in shaping the freedom of the projects. In a more direct manner, the experiments carried out in the

2 — Siza, Álvaro, *Imaginar a evidência*, Lisbon: Edições 70, 2000.

series of lost projects we started with directly fuel the projects we work on today. Even when the project is built the building only acts as a three-dimensional conclusion, a festive epilogue that both brings together and contradicts all these flat drawings. Each circle becomes a distorted ellipse, each color becomes a relative of itself, all references vanish for an instant.

Thus the project starts from the opposition of two canvases that challenge each other: the built context on the one hand and the white page on the other. The tension between the two is never fully resolved. Ideas coming from one might make little sense in the other, but their suppression would only sterilize the endeavor.

White walls are both a supremely affordable construction principle and the physical manifestation of the white canvas. They allow for everyday life and architectural elements to find their place and cohabit. They are spatial structure, but they are also light in every way.

Because it strategically dictates this division of space the floor plan is thus a crucial drawing. It sets the lines on which notes might take place. As many notes as the desired expression requires, not more, not less. As much patterned wood, mirrors and colored marble as the budget allows, no more, no less. And when even these aren't affordable, paint always works. A narrow budget shouldn't be a condemnation of romanticized frugality. Happy buildings have bones, but also full bellies and cheeky faces. An architecture of the minimum is an architecture of death.

So we search for a vitality of the present. Nostalgic prolonging of the context and pseudo-futuristic icons are equally stale to us. Still, these two paths are slowly becoming the only "acceptable" options in contemporary architectural production. The first one is valued for its innocuity, the second for symbolic exceptions which ultimately solidify the first. In these conditions we've been looking for safe havens of architectural expression. Interiors, suburbia, courtyards, etc. "B-sides" of the city where one can build in a relieving state of indifference towards past and future. Isn't that being modern?

Following that pursuit, many of the façades we've designed so far are hidden behind renovations of ordinary townhouses. As street façades are controlled and protected by the authorities, kept as fossils for touristic scenography, they become the conceptual back of our projects. On the other hand, the new façades, facing the inner side of the urban blocks, become assumed paradoxes. Both celebratory and marginal, they are exotic to what surrounds them, they irritate the urban fabric and ask for a reaction. They refuse to shy away.

The vast majority of our clients are like the vast majority of people. They have no specific interest in architecture, sometimes even a radical skepticism towards the figure of the architect. That's perfectly alright. In fact, most of our clients have never heard of "fala" and refer to us by our individual names alone. They reach us because they need paperwork with signatures and often come to us holding a catalogue of houses and point to the one they want. We could go down that road but we somehow enjoy the tougher life. We create our own windmills and each project ends up as a firework of stubborn desires, a fight in which everybody wins. Our architecture is unsolicited.

Being in a state of uninterrupted production, we are fast in many ways: energy and speed are vital. Our projects are generally modest in scale, so we run an economy of quantity. We have to think fast, submit, build, and move forward. A permanent state of emergency imposed by a precise economical context, limits and restraints that allows us to take advantage of challenging clients, imperfect contractors and small budgets.

Functional kitchens and a lot of built-in storage have to find a place within wider disciplinary intentions. A big percentage of our time and energy is dedicated to defending the bare existence of a project. The endless kitchen and the capricious column have to find a common ground, even if just for an instant. The only thing we cannot do is suppress the moment when ideas are thrown into a tangible future, searching for coherence. Furthermore, regulations, scale and a scarcity of financial means should never hinder the ambition of the project, nor be an excuse to normalize the proposal. Each bathroom renovation deserves as much intelligence, tenderness and freedom as the largest institution. Perhaps more. We once devoted two months of full-time work to the design of a birdhouse.

Of course, this method doesn't always pay off and comes with a good deal of frustrating moments and necessary plot twists. Some clients are allergic to pink or want their white to be beige. Imperfections are celebrated, some mistakes are planned and some are pure improvisation. We learn and unlearn every day, decide to forget what we were taught in architecture school, but can one truly decide to forget anything? Projects we love are regularly thrown in the trash bin. But more often than not they leave place for even more lovable ones. In short, we have to be resilient and stubborn. Being optimistic is a burden and communication isn't easy. It should never be easy. After all, we repeat words that aren't ours. Here Alessandro Bosetti's words come to mind: "I am repeating, gloriously repeating. As Beckett puts it: failing, trying again, failing better."[3]

3 — Bosetti, Alessandro, *Royals* (Monotype Records, 2010).

Biography

fala

fala is a naïve architecture practice. Founded in 2013 and based in Porto, it is led by Filipe Magalhães (Porto, 1987), Ana Luisa Soares (Porto, 1988) and Ahmed Belkhodja (Lausanne, 1990).

fala has taught and lectured at various universities and institutions throughout the world, and its work has been exhibited and published extensively. Both hedonistic and restrained, the atelier takes lightness and joy very seriously.

Past and present collaborators

Julia Andreychenko, Beatriz Branco, Chiara Carraro, Sajoua Ettarhi, Costanza Favero, Nina Guyot, Kentaro Hayashi, Jack Huang, Christina Kavoura, Gabriela Králová, Francesca Lantieri, Ricardo Leitão, Ana Lima, Jacopo Lugli, Anna Murisasco, Thea Orderud, Clara Pailler, Diogo Paixão, Carina Pannatier, Rute Peixoto, Camelia Petre, Francisco Rocha, Lera Samovich, Rikke Sandbugt, Elisa Sassi, Joana Sendas, Ana Sevo, Mariana Silva, Paulo Sousa, Jana Von Wyl, and Anyana Zimmermann.